Nostalgic
Nottingham

The publishers would like to thank the following companies for their support in the production of this book

Main sponsor
Hopwells Limited

Boots

Caunton Engineering Ltd

Halls Locksmiths Ltd

Hawthornes Printers

Luxfer Gas Cylinders

A.W. Lymn

Myford Ltd

Perfectos Speciality Inks Ltd

John Pye & Sons Ltd

Sandicliffe Garage Limited

H Sladen & Son Ltd

Spring Lane Farm Shop

GB Willbond Limited

First published in Great Britain by True North Books Limited
England HX3 6AE
01422 344344

ISBN 978 - 1906649289

Text, design and origination by True North Books

Nostalgic
Nottingham

CONTENTS

INTRODUCTION

If you would like to return to the St Ann's Well Road of a century ago and spend a couple of guineas at Hopewell's furniture store, then the opportunity will soon be yours. Similarly, those who enjoy reminiscing will have fun talking about the days when Queen Victoria looked down from her perch and across Market Square. Elsewhere, we can go back to when Pearson's department store stood on Long Row, next to Henry Farmer's music shop. Remember buying the sheet music for Doris Day's 'Whatever will be, will be' so that we could have a singsong around the piano in the parlour? There were times when we waited patiently on the platform at Victoria Station, ready to climb aboard a seaside special. But all these and more are just memories now. Thankfully, we have such publications as this, the latest from the True North series, that enables us to relive those periods in the last century when the pace of life was so different. They were days when sights and sounds provided other stimuli and when expectations and standards differed from those of modern society.

When you turn the first pages of 'Nostalgic Nottingham' be prepared for a trip down memory lane to a city that we might recall from our childhood. It is one that our parents and grandparents told us about and is preserved by virtue of glorious photographs and captions that are at times poignant and at others wry or thought provoking. Our city has a wonderful history. Mention of it in Saxon times saw it develop as a homestead in the area that became the Lace Market. In the days of the Vikings, we were one of the five burghs or fortified towns that made up the Danelaw. The 11th century castle was the focus for a settlement that grew around it and no mention of Nottingham would be complete without reference to Robin Hood, the legendary figure who inspired dozens of tales, several television series and a number of movies.

In the middle of the 15th century, Nottingham became a sort of self governing county corporate and continued to grow in importance during the Industrial Revolution as a prosperous centre for the textile trade, with the manufacture of lace predominating. Many fine Victorian buildings date from these days of prosperity, with structures designed by Alfred Waterhouse, TC Hine and Watson Fothergill being of particular importance. Companies such as Boots pharmaceuticals, Raleigh cycles and John Player's tobacco products were founded here. During the 20th century, Vision Express, Speedo sportswear and Serif software have all contributed to the local economy. The delights of 'Nostalgic Nottingham' now await the reader as the initial leaves of the book are turned.

Welcome to a world where trams formerly clanked and bobbies waved traffic across junctions as they stood on point duty. As well as the happy memories, there are the sad times and uncomfortable moments to be recalled. Not everything in our background was sweetness and light. We endured the privations and horrors of global wars, the poverty in the slums and the belt tightening days of the Depression when so many had to live from hand to mouth. But, in those difficult times, the bulldog spirit and sense of hope brought us through. Share now in those moments when we worked and laughed together and, best of all, played together. They were times when we could make some of our own entertainment and did not have to rely on others to create it for us. It is only modern youth that cries out that there is nowhere to go and nothing to do. We devised our own games, provided our own pleasures. They were occasions when grass was something to play on rather than smoke and when men smiled at a pretty girl and wished her 'Good morning' without being accused of harassment. The companies and organisations which have developed and thrived in the city over the recent decades are many. We take pleasure in including in this book histories of an outstanding selection of different companies whose contribution to the development and sustainability of the city's economic prosperity is a matter of record. With their co-operation and access to their respective photographic archives, we have been able to tell their stories and hopefully trigger the memories of local people who have worked for them or been touched by their part in community life. Dean Martin sang 'Memories are made of this' and how right he was. As modern waitresses now say, 'Enjoy'.

TEXT	ANDREW MITCHELL, TONY LAX
PHOTOGRAPH COMPILATION	TONY LAX
DESIGNER	SEAMUS MOLLOY
BUSINESS DEVELOPMENT EDITOR	PETER PREST

EDWARDIAN NOTTINGHAM

Showing the eastern aspect of Market Place from Angel Row on a market day in 1910. Looking along Long Row, with Market Street off to the left. Also featured is the triangular area known as the Pot Market in the centre foreground. The Queen Victoria statue, erected by public subscription, is to the right. The statue was unveiled in July 1905, in a ceremony by the Duchess of Portland. The grand old lady was moved almost 50 years later, with much care, to a new site.

Below: This view shows the statue of Queen Victoria and the lily pond. It originally stood in Old Market Square on Beast Market Hill and was moved to the memorial gardens in 1953. In 1920 Jesse Boot purchased, and presented to the City, 36 acres of open land that lay along the northern side of the Victoria Embankment alongside the River Trent, opposite Plaisaunce Jesse Boot's summer house which was demolished in 1961. The 'New Park' was laid out with grass and trees, and provided a barrier against flooding as well as a pleasant walkway alongside the river. As part of the development an imposing war memorial gateway was built, with the aid of funds from Jesse Boot. The gardens were opened on 11 November 1927.

Above: The Nottingham Bicycle Club was open for membership to both sexes, though the ladies had to be careful in their attire so as not to reveal a dainty ankle in case it sent male pulses racing. The variety of cycles chosen by this group suggests that

they may have been on some form of rally, rather than just out for a leisurely spin. A history of bikes and trikes from the first popular ones of the 1860s, through to the latest models seen here

in around 1900, is encompassed in the photograph taken at Bottesford, in the Vale of Belvoir. John Dunlop's invention of the pneumatic tyre in 1888 helped usher in a golden age of cycling in the closing years of the 19th century. Add to this the introduction of cable operated brakes, a rear free wheel and derailleur gears around the turn into the last century and cycling became easier and horizons were widened considerably. Of course, Nottingham has had a major interest in two wheeled transport ever since the Raleigh company was established in the city.

Left: In 1887 Sir Frank Bowden purchased an interest in a small bicycle company on Raleigh Street in Nottingham. Taking its name from the street the Raleigh Bicycle Company was formed in 1890. It was the site of a small workshop which was occupied throughout the 20th century and started producing diamond-frame safety bicycles at the rate of three a week. Within just six years it had grown to be the world's leading cycle manufacturer. The factory covered a seven and a half acre site on Faraday Road. Its founder, Frank Bowden (1848-1921) was already enormously wealthy, having made his pile on the stock market in the early 1870s. He was given a baronetcy in 1915.

Right: The Edwardian period is often regarded as a romantic Golden Age of long summer afternoons, garden parties and big hats. This cultural perception was created by those that remembered the Edwardian age with nostalgia looking back to their childhood across the vast, dark, horrid abyss of the Great War. Fashion in European countries continued the long elegant lines of the 1890s. Tall, stiff collars characterise the period, as do women's broad hats and full Gibson girl" hairstyles. Blouses and dresses were full in front and puffed into a "pigeon breast" shape with a narrow waist that was often accented with a sash or belt.

Skirts brushed the floor, often with a train, even for day dresses, in mid-decade. Not long after this picture was taken the fashion houses of Paris began to show a new silhouette, with a thicker waist, flatter bust, and narrower hips. By the end of the decade the most fashionable skirts cleared the floor and approached the ankle. Frothy washable day dresses of translucent cotton, called lingerie dresses, were worn in warm climates. Giving a pictorial example of the fashion of the day in Nottingham are; Mabel, Bertha and Zillah Rowe, three daughters of Walter and Elizabeth Rowe. Walter Rowe was a boot maker and repairer based at Kingston Road, Sneinton.

Right: Viewed from the southeast, looking from Hollowstone along Stoney Street, St Mary's Churchyard can be seen on the left. The church on Low Pavement is thought to be the third on this site and dates from 1474. It is an example of the early English Perpendicular style of architecture. Many of the women we can see were lace workers. Nowadays, the Lace Market area is a trendy place, with smart bars and restaurants fronting cobbled streets. Nottingham's famous industry owed much to a couple of major innovations. The traditional craft was but a modest cottage industry until William Lee invented a framework knitting

machine in 1589. This enabled a much greater volume of lace to be produced than ever before. When, in 1808, John Heathcoate introduced a hand operated machine, the modern industry really took off. The demand from fashionable ladies for the finely worked, delicate products almost exceeded supply. Lace was the symbol of good living and an elegant life style. But, times change, as does fashion. In the 20th century, the demand for synthetics fibres that could be easily cared for was on the increase. As with many things in the modern world, expediency replaced good taste. The downward spiral for the lace industry was accelerated by the Second World War and struggled to make any sort of impression. Some of the old Victorian machines, however, are still in use today and are often interfaced with computers.

the greater freedom of the Edwardian era. The mood was partly set by the monarch. Instead of the dour image displayed by Queen Victoria towards the end of her reign, we now had the jolly persona of her son. He was a bit of a rascal, but an amusing sort, nonetheless. The population was determined to move forward in these exciting times. Gas lighting illuminated our streets and homes, making them such cheerier places. Electricity hummed though wires and cables, introducing us to a powerful tool that would, in the not too distant future, transform our homes even further. Outside, we could already use this power source to support our public transport with the provision of tramways. We had heard that a couple of American brothers were close to a breakthrough with powered flight. We

Above: There were some happy, smiling faces aboard the horse drawn bus as it crossed Trent Bridge in 1906. Some of them had been well scrubbed with the Sunlight soap being advertised on the coachwork. Britons were looking forward to the new century and what it might hold for them. Already they were experiencing

had already seen the first motor cars on the roads and there was talk of building huge, unsinkable ocean going liners. Our wonderful Empire occupied a fifth of the globe and there was a lot to be said for being British.

Bottom left: An unusual photograph from 1907 showing children with their toys, which are modest by today's standards. The toys are a traditional selection, such as snakes and ladders, train sets, a car (unusual at this early date), dolls, Steiff teddy bears, whistle/flute, drum, a model horse and cart and a boat. The boy at the front on the right seems to be holding what looks like a real dog and the little girl right at the back is on a rocking horse. Presumably, they were allowed to bring toys into school on a special occasion. Around this time, the welfare of children was improving, largely due to the Growing 1906 Education (Provision of Meals) Act and the 1907 Education Act. Up to this point the provision of school meals had been haphazard and many schools relied on voluntary work to provide meals to children from poor backgrounds. This initiative gave local authorities the right to assist those providing voluntary meals services to schools. The Education Administrative Provisions Act introduced, for the first time, a schools medical service. School children were to be medically inspected on a regular basis and minor ailments were treated. The annual report received by the Chief Medical Officer clearly showed the lack of good health amongst children from poor backgrounds. This Act allowed for the earlier discovery of disease and the potential treatment at an earlier stage.

Above and below: This view shows motor car competitors lined up for judging at the Midlands Industrial Exhibition in 1904. This Indian Raj, Empire style pavilion was opened in May 1903. The Industrial Hall had two floors with 50,000 square feet of space. Other attractions included a Canadian water chute 100 ft high with a slope and dip of 600ft, a maze, Fairy River with a lane of stalactites a mile long, brilliantly illuminated with all the bright and rich colours of a giant array of prisms, distorting mirrors, an American roller coaster and Concert Hall. Unfortunately, the pavilion burnt down just over a year later due to an electrical short circuit. The building was gutted and the fire spread to the Nottingham Forest Football Club pavilion, which was also destroyed.

Above: At the start of the last century, moving house was just as traumatic an event as it is today. Thomas Gray was one of the city's specialists in getting your belongings from one address to another, utilising all of the modern facilities available to the Edwardian. It looks to have been something of a Little and Large company, if the nature of the massive steam wagon and the tiny horse and cart are to be representative. Perhaps the small contraption was used to move a doll's house. Seen on Cope Street at the junction with Palin Street, the removal contractor was someone who became important in the late Victorian era. Until the mid 19th century, it was common for successive generations of a family to live their whole lives within a small radius. But, with the coming of the railway and the spread of the industrial revolution, people moved many miles away from where they had been brought up. Instead of carrying belongings a few hundred yards if moving house, this now became a matter of a major upheaval. Initially, contractors used strong horses and large carts or vans to help provide an efficient service. The steam engine, so popular on the railway, was adapted by some as a road vehicle that could challenge the horse as a means of pulling power. Thomas Rickett built a steam carriage in 1858, while the small road steamer that HP Holt introduced in 1866 was capable of reaching 20 mph. By the 1870s, large steam vehicles capable of carrying a dozen passengers were in production and it only needed simple adjustments in design to create steam wagons and vans.

Below: St Peter's Church is one of three places of worship in the city that date back to medieval times. The original church, built in 1100, was destroyed in a fire, but elements of its 1180 replacement can be traced within its present walls. St Peter's Square, as seen in this photograph taken from Wheelergate in c1890, was marshland until the middle of the 18th century. A stream ran along the west side of the churchyard. The first church served the French or Norman quarter of the city, while those of Saxon stock favoured St Mary's. The magnificent spire and tower are thought to date from 1340. The church was damaged by bombardment during the Civil War and various restoration works were carried out in the years that followed. One of its major building projects took place in 1877 when the chancel and north transept were created. St James' Room, adjoining the 1815 vestry, was added in 1936, three years after St James' Church on Standard Hill closed and the congregation largely moved here. In more recent times, St Peter's Square was widened when, in 1965, part of the churchyard was sacrificed.

THE WAR YEARS

Below: In 1944, if the Germans had landed near Hull they might just have managed to make it as far downstream as Nottingham. In this unlikely scenario, we had men ready to deal with the situation. The river patrol on the Trent was ready and waiting. More seriously, such exercises could have come in handy for D-Day landings. The waters of the English Channel were much more difficult to negotiate, but there were some similarities with boarding and disembarking a patrol boat on the Trent. This group had its links with the Home Guard, the doughty set of men who were pledged to defend our towns in case of invasion. The unit in the photograph was based at Gunthorpe and covered an area from Sawley right through to the Humber estuary. These chaps and their activities provided the inspiration for the popular TV sitcom, 'Dad's

Army'. Those who had actually served in the Home Guard were not amused by the antics of Captain Mainwaring's platoon, seeing the programme as an insult to the dedication of those who had been ready to put their lives on the line in the service of their country.

Right: On 8 May 1945 all Britain took to the streets. After nearly six long years the war in Europe was over. All at once the drab years were forgotten. The shortages no longer mattered. A blaze of multi coloured flags, fireworks and decorations celebrated the great day. This scene in the Old Market Square was repeated in every town and city centre in the land. In our back streets, party hats were hurriedly made and the children given a treat the like they had not known since the 1930s. Some women shed a quiet

tear for the sweetheart or father who would not be coming home. For each one who looked forward to the day she would be reunited with her husband there was another who knew that hers lay in a foreign field. All the same, people went mad and all inhibitions were cast aside. They hugged total strangers and kissed policemen. Massive hokey cokeys snaked along Poultry and Cheapside and we all rejoiced together. Similar scenes were repeated two months later when the war with Japan ended. Then we really could start to build a future for our children. Let's have three cheers for our brave lads overseas. In London, the King and Queen made repeated appearances on the balcony at Buckingham Palace in scenes of national fervour the likes of which had never before been witnessed.

Below right: War had been declared, and every citizen of Britain, young and old, male and female, was called upon to put his or her back into the war effort. Those who did not go into military service of one kind or another worked in factories, dug for victory, gave up their tin baths and aluminium saucepans, joined organisations and aided in any way they could. These boys were not going to be left out; they might be too young to fight but while there were sandbags to be filled they were going to do their bit to protect their school building.

Bottom: When the First World War began in the summer of 1914, many people regarded it as little more than a skirmish that would be over by Christmas. It was with high anticipation of a swift conclusion that friends and family waved goodbye to the troops leaving Victoria Station in September 1914. Here, men of the Sherwood Foresters said farewell to loved ones as they left to join the British Expeditionary Force in France. The 2nd Battalion was rushed into action almost immediately, taking part in bitter fighting in the Battle of the Aisne. A bloody introduction to trench warfare was part of the soldiers' learning curve. After a week in which no quarter was given or taken, the battalion carried out an attack to plug a gap in the lines. About a quarter of the 1,000 men in the manoeuvre were killed. Both the 1st and 2nd Battalions of the Foresters served with distinction on French soil throughout the war. Several men, including Privates Rivers and Bees and Corporals Upton and Beet, won Victoria Crosses.

There were countless other instances of bravery that were recognised by medals and special mention. Many of those who marched off that day nearly a century ago never returned, but they are not forgotten.

Top right: When it appeared that war would be likely, the country began preparing itself for the worst. Civil defence groups practised what they would do in the event of an aerial attack. The general public was well aware from newsreel footage of the

devastation that could be wreaked by the Luftwaffe. During the Second World War, Nottingham suffered from enemy air raids but to a lesser extent than many cities of comparable size. A major air raid on the city occurred on the night of 8 May, 1941, and among the buildings destroyed were several at the southeastern corner of Friar Lane. Except for minor blast damage, Nottingham Building Society's offices, situated just 50 yards away, escaped virtually unscathed. When it came to civil defence Britain had to rely on a variety of ordinary people to take over duties that would normally have been the remit of hardened professionals. Air Raid Precautions (ARP) were handed over to civilians, some of whom were in reserved occupations. This group, seen in late 1938 were kitted out in gas masks and protective gear as they carried out an exercise that would be done for real in a year or so's time.

Below left: A Moot Hall was the name given to early town halls, used for various civic and public purposes, and sometimes as courts. Nottingham's used to stand in Friar Lane. This scene of wreckage shows what was left of the Moot Hall and its neighbour H Wilkinson & Co after the night of 8th-9th May, 1941. The mock-Georgian Moot Hall which has just been reduced to rubble was built around 1900. It replaced an earlier Moot Hall, a 17th century building which had formerly served as one of Nottingham's old inns, known as The Feathers. By contrast, the hall which took its place was to serve the city for barely four decades before being wiped out by enemy action. But the citizens of Nottingham had more to worry about than the loss of their Moot Hall. During the night the emergency services had been called out to around a hundred fires; six rest centres were very busy coping with the 1,286 people who had been bombed out; and there were casualties to be taken care of. Doubtless the horror of the raid left Nottingham shocked and saddened, and perhaps trying to draw some small comfort from the knowledge that but for the 'starfish site' at Cropwell Butler, the consequences might have been even worse; fires lit here as a decoy had succeeded in fooling almost a hundred enemy bombers, who dropped their bombs on the open countryside instead of Nottingham.

Below centre: It was possibly the acute wartime shortages of food and supplies which made doctors, health workers and mothers alike very aware of the health of the new generation, and children were carefully weighed, measured and immunised against the illnesses that had at one time meant disfigurement or even death. A vaccine for polio, the scourge of former years which left behind its terrible mark of wasted and useless limbs, only came later, however. American scientist Jonas Edward Salk developed a vaccine in 1955, and an oral vaccine was produced in 1960. The vaccines brought the dreaded disease under control and today polio is rarely seen. On a day to day basis, vitamins were vital to the health of children, and long before the advent of the cod liver oil capsule, the recommended spoonful of cod liver oil was administered to the youngest children every day in schools and nurseries around the country during the 1940s. Children

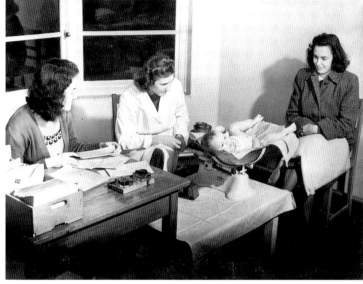

might have screwed up their noses at the fishy taste, but the nourishing cod liver oil went a long way towards keeping them healthy. The vitamin-packed orange juice was far more palatable, and artful mothers would often use the orange juice as a bribe: no cod liver oil, no orange juice. Following hard on the heels of the oil, the juice took away the distinctive taste that was disliked by so many children.

Below: Say 'wartime parades' and the words conjure up the tramp of heavy boots, the gleam of polished buttons, and perhaps even the glint of weapons; but this is a parade of a slightly different nature. The occasion pictured here is the Joint Church Parade of the Red Cross and St John Ambulance Brigade at St Mary's Church, during 1940. These two organisations gave admirable service during the second world war. Not only were they constantly exposed to the trauma of dealing with casualties who

had suffered terrible injuries, but they were also called upon to attend disasters where they sometimes had to be prepared to risk their own lives in order to search for survivors or fatalities in the wreckage after an explosion, when fire or the presence of gas made the situation hazardous. Nottingham had twelve First Aid Posts and three mobile first aid units; the rule of thumb was that there should be one FAP to every 15,000 people. FAPs were manned by a doctor, a trained nurse and nursing auxiliaries. First Aid Parties were composed of four men and a driver, all experienced first-aid workers trained by the Red Cross, the St John Ambulance or St Andrew's Society. Thanks to their bravery and their devotion, over and above the call of duty, suffering and loss of life was minimised. We take great pleasure in including this photograph in our collection.

Above: The crowds standing around with luggage might almost have been setting off on a pleasure trip, were it not for the arm-bands which identify them as evacuees. Evacuations during WW2 were organised by a special Emergency Committee. Sometimes evacuees were simply moved out of

their homes in the city to the nearby countryside, which we think was the case in this photograph, but sometimes they had to travel much further. In all, around 5,000 were evacuated from Nottingham itself, and though most went to towns and villages in Nottinghamshire, some were sent to other counties. Children from London and the densely-populated areas in the South East could expect to be scattered all over the country; some cities even sent their children abroad. As can be imagined, all this led to a glorious mix of accents, social backgrounds and lifestyles in the parts of Britain which were receiving evacuees; children who had grown up in the Nottinghamshire countryside got to know children from inner cities who had never seen a cow before. For most people involved in the evacuation programme, the experience was on the whole positive, though some unfortunately had a miserable and traumatic time of it - and probably nobody enjoyed the first few moments at their new home, when to add to the emotional uncertainty, the new arrivals had to be subjected to a thorough inspection for nits, lice and other such uninvited guests.

ROYAL VISITS

Below and bottom right: Seen here on 24 June, 1914, the King and Queen are in a procession along Albert Street towards Wheeler Gate and on to the Market Place. The visit was part of a Royal Progress tour of Nottinghamshire for a few days. During his visit to Retford it was reported the King looked very tired on this heavy schedule. This is hardly surprising as it should be remembered that these visits were only a few weeks before the outbreak of World War 1, which would have been playing on his mind. Notice the premises of the City and Suburban Window Cleaning Company top centre of picture.

Facing page, bottom: A picture of women window cleaners working for City and Suburban Window Cleaning Company during the First World War. The war was often said to be responsible for the immediate postwar feminist reforms in Britain, and undoubtedly it helped as it did give women the opportunity to show that they could do what they had long claimed.

Top right: Narrow Marsh developed on the south side of Nottingham in a low-lying area by the River Leen. Along with Broad Marsh, it expanded into one of the most densely-populated parts of the city. By the end of the 19th century, the area was notorious for its network of overcrowded yards and alleys. The major cholera outbreak of 1832 killed many locals and this was touched on in a speech made by the Prince of Wales, the

THE ROYAL VISIT TO NOTTINGHAM,

future King Edward VIII, during a visit to Narrow Marsh made exactly a century later. He found time to honour the 44th Nottingham (Leenside) Company of Girl Guides with part of his time and the girls provided him with a guard of honour. Guiding had become remarkably popular in just a short time. After Baden Powell introduced his 'Scouting for Boys' in 1908, he held a rally at Crystal Palace the following year to be attended by members of the Scout movement he had initiated on Brownsea Island. He was amazed to find that the rally had been gatecrashed by a number of girls who demanded that he form a similar organisation for them. At first he refused, but soon gave in to the tremendous pressure imposed upon him. His sister, Agnes was charged with the creation of the Girl Guide movement. By 1910, there were 6,000 enrolled and the numbers snowballed as the years passed.

Thousands filled Old Market Place, making use of every vantage point possible. They squashed up behind crash barriers, stood on tiptoe and hung out of windows and across balconies. It was just a sea of people. Union flags were unfurled and banners stretched across buildings. Children waved their own little flags on sticks and the cheering was heard right across the

city. On 28 June, 1949, Princess Elizabeth and the Duke of Edinburgh arrived in a limousine that was part of a long motorcade holding dignitaries who were assembled to mark the quincentenary celebrations to remember the charter granted by King Henry II in 1449. That formal document granted borough status to Nottingham. Our future Queen and her husband had travelled from Edinburgh on the royal train, spending the previous night in a siding just outside Nottingham. Attired in a floral dress, she was as pretty as a picture on a chocolate box. The Princess was conducting one of the first of a series of engagements held since the birth of her first child the previous November. In addition to the official business in the Council House, the royal couple visited the grounds at The Forest. There they were entertained by a display of dancing performed by local schoolchildren. The Duke was already becoming accustomed to walking a couple of paces behind his wife. This was a position he would continue to adopt for the next 60 years and more. We knew that the young woman who honoured our city in 1949 would one day be our monarch. However, the time was upon us sooner than we all expected. Her father, George VI, died less than three years after this visit and Princess Elizabeth took over a throne that she was to grace with her elegance well into the next century.

Above: The crowds stood obediently behind the crash barriers as they welcomed Princess Margaret to Old Market Square. She was on her way into the Council House for a civic reception in her honour. The visit was made in July 1970 as part of the celebrations for the Nottingham Festival. Our royal guest was escorted by Councillor Oscar Watkinson, the Lord Mayor. Dressed very fashionably, the princess was something of lady with an eye for the gentlemen. Born in 1930, she was as much of a rebel as her sister, the future Queen Elizabeth II was a conformist. In the early postwar years she was very much a party animal, featuring in the gossip columns of the day. She found love with former Group Captain Peter Townsend, her father's equerry. He was a divorcé and deemed by the establishment as an unsuitable husband. Margaret was forced to abandon him and never again found true love. She married the former Antony Armstrong-Jones in 1960, but divorced in 1978. She dallied with

a number of other men, several many years her junior, and died in 2002 without ever finding true happiness. Her latter years were plagued with illness and the aftermath of injuries received when scalded in a bathroom accident. Her mood swings, that veered from utter charm to complete boorishness in a matter of moments, perplexed even her closest friends.

Below: This lady has been a regular and most welcome visitor over the years, both as a Princess and as our Queen. Seen on Lenton Boulevard in May, 1968, she was paying a visit to the Raleigh cycle works, escorted by the company chairman, Leslie Roberts. She seemed thoroughly delighted to be out and about, meeting her public. The workers were granted time off to greet their special guest and they gave her a right, royal welcome. They appreciated the way in which the Queen was travelling, riding in an open topped car so that she could be closer to her subjects. She was actually going against the advice of those charged with her security. Ever since President Kennedy was gunned down in Dallas in 1963, bodyguards became ever more twitchy. Their equilibrium was not helped by the assassination of Martin Luther King a month before this photographed visit. It would be even more sorely tested a few weeks hence, as it was then that Bobby Kennedy was shot dead in Los Angeles. Public figures have become more vulnerable to such incidents in latter years. Two Popes and Ronald Reagan were both injured and John Lennon was killed by gunmen with no sane reason to carry out such acts. Even Queen Elizabeth was shot at during the 1981 Trooping the Colour ceremony and her daughter, Princess Anne, was lucky to escape a kidnap attempt by an armed attacker in 1974.

STREETS OF CHANGE

An elevated view looking towards the West Bridgford side of the River Trent. In this 1912 picture Trent Bridge tram terminus is next to the Town Arms Hotel. The tram on the right is on route for the Market Place and the second tram looks to be heading towards Bulwell. In the good old days, Nubolic disinfectant soap was used in conjunction with hydrochloric shampoo and chlorine toothpaste. It was advertised as 'promoting health' and 'ensuring sweetness'.

Above: A 1915 image showing the exchange fish stall in the foreground. The 'Exchange' (top of picture) was completed in 1726 but, by 1815, it needed considerable repair and remodelling. In 1877, the Corporation decided to move from the old Council House in Weekday Cross, but, their needs were not satisfied and they soon had to use temporary accommodation, for Council matters. In the year of their move, the corporation found that further repairs and alterations were necessary on the 'Exchange' and, work was carried out to remodel and reinstate the building, The idea of a new complex was approved by the Council in December 1924 and the contract was let in May 1925. The Council House now stands on this site which was once part of Nottinghams 'great Market Place' where, from medieval times, right through to the 1920s a Saturday market was held here as well as the October 'Goose Fair' which, in the 19th Century became a fun fair. Street names like The Poultry, Cheapside and Beastmarket Hill recall the use of the area as a market. The banner ('Every man is needed, why do the single men stay behind?.. will not our women help us!'), was to rally citizens for the the war effort.

Below: Wilford is an attractive village, bordered on the north and west by the River Trent. Somewhat ghoulishly, it has a macabre claim to fame in that one Jeremiah Brandreth, probably no relation to Giles, was, in the early 19th century, the last person to be decapitated for treason. Apparently, he was born here in 1790 and was later part of a revolutionary group that had the foolish plan of storming the Tower of London in 1817. Thoughts of insurrection were not uppermost in the minds of these lads, pedalling through the floodwater of yet another breach of its banks by the River Trent. It has a history of flooding that is recorded as far back as medieval times. Despite the raising of bank levels, the building of sluices, the cutting of channels and other measures taken in attempt to lessen the effects of Mother Nature, the old lady usually wins out. Not that these schoolboys seemed bothered. They appear to be enjoying the challenge of staying upright. Perhaps they had confidence in their bikes. Hopefully, they had supported local industry and purchased Raleighs. The Trent is unusual among British rivers in that it flows north for a major part of its route and also possesses a tidal bore, the 'Trent Aegir'.

Right: Looking East during the re-laying of the tramlines, which were moved at the time that the 'slabs' were laid out in the new Market Square. The construction of the Council House here in 1929 is almost complete, along with the laying out and paving of the Old Market Square and Processional Way. Long Row Central to the left, shows Griffin and Spalding, later to become Debenham's.

Below: A scene of tremendous activity is shown in this picture from 1929. By this time the new Council House had been completed and looked out in all its white splendour on the ant-like figures below. The major project underway involved the re-laying of the tram tracks and around 50 workmen can be seen engaged in the mammoth task while a dozen or so foremen and supervisors look on. It is a sobering thought to remember that the workmen had little or no access to labour-saving tools, even in the late 1920s. Most of the work they did was achieved through the sweat of their brow which makes their achievements all the more impressive.

Right: Watson Fothergill designed many of our most notable buildings. The son of a wealthy lace merchant, he was born in Mansfield in 1841 as Fothergill Watson. He reversed his name in order to retain links with the maternal side of his family. Influenced by the Gothic Revival and Old English Vernacular modes of architecture, the Queen's Chambers, built in 1897, on Long Row Central typified his style. It was completed in the year of Victoria's Diamond Jubilee. Other notable buildings included the Nottingham and Notts Bank, later the NatWest, on Thurland Street. This busy scene from 1924 also shows a number of successful businesses from the time, including Saxone shoes, Lyons Coffee House, the jeweller, H Samuel and Lipton's. At the end of the 19th century

Lipton was created by Sir Thomas Lipton in Glasgow. His enterprise soon flourished and he established a chain of grocers across Britain. Under the slogan "direct from the tea gardens to the tea pot", this entrepreneurial businessman wanted to make tea a popular and approachable drink for everyone. Next to Lipton's, The Picture House was showing a silent movie, 'The Merry Madcap'. This was a vehicle for Elsie Janis (1889-1956), the Ohio born singer and actress who was the sweetheart of the American forces in the First World War. She did a lot of work entertaining the troops and raising funds for Liberty Bonds. She was one of the first to go overseas to perform for soldiers serving on foreign shores. 'The Merry Madcap', the tale of a young convent girl who wanted to see the world before settling down, dated from 1915, but she was still a box office attraction throughout the interwar years. Her last film role was in 1940, alongside a young Peter Cushing.

There is something very pleasing about this 1932 view across Old Market Square, taken from the Council House. Its is a lunchtime scene yet all seems very tranquil, as Nottingham folk take advantage of the mid-day sunshine. The paving stone is so clean and litter free it is almost bleached white, a world away from the hustle and bustle of how it was up until the 1920s when it was used as a market area. The stone for the 'Market Square' (except for the paving stones which are silex stone) is Portland stone, from the Isle of Portland, off the south coast of Dorset; the quarry had been used by Christopher Wren when engaged on St. Paul's Cathedral, London, and churches elsewhere. One piece of stone, lying on the shore, left by Wren, was brought to Nottingham and used as the key stone of the Council House. If you happen to be within close proximity of the dome of the Council House, on the

hour, you will hear the strong toll of 'Little John' the striking bell which is reputed to be the deepest toned bell in the country; it weighs two and a half tons. The Market Square was the place where important pronouncements were made and doubled as a form of speakers' corner where people could let off steam by shouting the odds on various matters that concerned them.

We may bemoan the passing of time that has seen so many beautiful and/or historic buildings and streets scrapped or completely remodelled. However, there are some things about which we shed no tears. The poverty and deprivation of the Depression era, the slums and substandard living conditions our parents and grandparents endured and the hopeless plight in which many found themselves are best consigned to the past. Even so, it is important that we do not forget that they existed. Such pictures, as the one showing Narrow Marsh, Sussex Square, with its washing line hanging from the lampost by the tenements, capture the essence of life in 1934. It was tough. Nationally, millions were out of work and the welfare state was over a decade away. Living here, in crowded and insanitary surroundings, respiratory diseases shortened the life span of many inhabitants. The tenement windows are historically interesting. Known as 'frameknitter windows', they referred to the practice of many former residents who knitted stockings, gloves and hats at home. They often worked on frames kept upstairs and worked by an extra wide window that allowed as much light as possible to enter. The slum clearance programme of the mid 20th century flattened this area and the Broadmarsh Centre stands here now. Woburn Street, off Colwick Street, with its fruit and vegetable barrows, was another such depressed part of the city.

Above: Even the word 'outfitter' takes us back in time. It was the sort of term that remained as a popular alternative to tailor for many a year until even that word became unfashionable. Tuckley Brothers, by the junction of Parliament Square and Milton Street and across the way from the Milton's Head Hotel, was just such a supplier of male fashion. It was a fairly standard role in the early 1930s as men needed a suit for best and, if they were white collar workers, one for the office. Otherwise, that was about it. A bloke might buy a jacket and trousers for everyday use, plus a few shirts, but it was all practical stuff. The idea of fitting in with any trends or modes was laughable. There weren't any. That was left to the ladies. The policeman on point duty was having a busy day. Electrically operated traffic lights, first trialled in this country in Wolverhampton in 1927, only made their way onto Britain's city streets in any great numbers during the years either side of the last war. It was down to the humble bobby to keep town centres on the move. Like some well choreographed Marcel Marceau, he controlled the flow of everything from the humblest of cyclists to the largest of pantechnicons. With one imperious movement of an arm he could halt the mightiest of vehicles in its tracks.

Right: Jobs were scarce and money was tight for many families in the mid 1930s. Up in the North East, men from the Jarrow shipyards marched on London in an effort to highlight the privations being experienced by the working classes, especially in such traditional employment areas as mining and shipbuilding. But it was not just these jobs where the pinch was felt. It was right across the board. Families went hungry and made do with what they could. It was only in 1934 that the Unemployment

Assistance Board was created. However, benefits were minimal and those who were unemployed for lengthy periods became subject to the Poor Law, whereby people were forced to do service for scant rewards. Those unable to keep up with the rent were evicted and many felt the pain of despair that went hand in hand with hunger pangs. They sought out every possible chance to get the necessities at the cheapest possible cost. This opportunist mini market was held at the junction of Colwick Street and Cavendish Street, in one of the poorer parts of the city. Outside John Pownall's Marine Store, customers picked over second hand clothes that they might just be able to afford at knockdown prices.

Right: Exceptionally cold weather swept from Russia in March 1947 bringing snow and frost. As the snows melted, the River Trent burst its banks at Wilford and West Bridgford. The flood waters reached as far as Nottingham train station, and reached a record height of 79ft 4 in on the 19 February. Houses in Wilford had water up to second floor bedrooms. Army amphibious 'Duck' landing craft and Sea Scouts in boats helped evacuate people marooned in houses. 700 volunteers helped rescue and bring relief to those affected. This scene shows the River Trent flooded on to Colliery Road at the side of Wilford Power Station and Clifton Colliery. This area was later to become Queens Drive Retail Park.

Below: At a rough guess, Christmas was a-coming. A large array of turkeys hanging outside Davis's butcher's shop at 32 Carlton Road, Sneinton, makes it rather

obvious. At other times, with rabbits and hares hanging there, you could say that it gave the game away! We thought absolutely nothing of seeing recently slaughtered animals put on display so that they could gain some added flavour. The butcher wiped the blood from his hands onto his striped apron and cheekily asked the housewife what he could do for her today. It was a jolly game that they played out on a regular basis, without any care for so called harassment in the banter or health and safety issues in the way that the food was displayed. During the last war, it was the wise housewife who made a friend of the local butcher. He could always help the meat ration stretch a little further and could be relied upon to keep a special something or an extra egg or two under his counter, just for his favourite customers. The shop next door at No 30 belonged to Wood's corn and flour dealership.

Right: This is not an example of the Lambeth Walk, but of the Exchange Walk. The photograph was taken there on 16 December, 1938. With little more than a week's shopping to go before Christmas morning dawned, it was little wonder that the shops were full and the

pavements crowded as parents searched for that special little item that would top off a child's stocking. Looking north from St Peter's Gate, these shoppers appreciated that their sons would be happy to get gifts of Dinky cars, Meccano sets or Hornby trains. Tomboy daughters would thrill to receive a model steam engine whose little boiler was fired by igniting methylated spirit that had an odour and purplish colour all of its own. Their more traditional sisters were delighted with a doll or some pretty hair ribbons. How different it is for parents now. It is not a case of buying something the kids will enjoy, but of keeping up with the neighbours who spend an obscene amount on a myriad of electronic gadgets, most of which will be discarded by New Year. However, what the mums and dads in 1938 did not realise was that this was to be the last Christmas for some time when we really could think of peace to all men. In a year from then, Hitler's jackbooted armies were sweeping across Europe and his pilots were strafing people below from their Messerschmitts.

Below: This 1958 image of Carlton Street is looking east towards Goose Gate, with the junction with George Street on the left. Carlton Street obtained its present name at the beginning of the 19th century. Prior to that time it had been called Swine Green, which relates back to a more agricutural Nottingham when just about everybody kept swine, and infact pigsties were a common sight throughout the town. On the left can be seen J&H Bell Ltd, printers, stationers and bookseller. On the opposite corner is The George Hotel, which was built around 1823, and was originally named The King George IV Inn. Over the years it has had a number of owners including The Duke of Rutland. The hotel has seen many famous guests including Charles Dickens, Elizabeth Taylor and Richard Burton. Today it is part of the Comfort Hotel chain.

Below: The double decker bus headed off to Market Square along Albert Street. Seen from St Peter's Church, looking towards Lister Gate, shoppers were out in force on 30 July 1949. Although the people on the streets did not know it at the time, this was the day when the dirty word 'communism' became a reality and not just an ideology we had heard about. Thousands of miles away, on the other side of the world, a British frigate, HMS Amethyst, was acting as a guard vessel for the British Embassy in Chinese Nanking, close to the Yangtze River. With a civil war raging between the Nationalists and Communists, this was a dangerous time for neutrals. In late April, the Amethyst came under fire from forces supporting the latter cause. There a number of casualties and the vessel became grounded in river mud. However, it was refloated, but remained under Chinese guard for three months until the captain and crew decided upon a daring escape. The ship slipped its anchor and made a dash for freedom down river, braving the battery of guns lined up on the banks on either side of the river. The story of the successful freedom run was on the front pages of the newspapers these Nottingham citizens read the following morning. The event was made into a popular movie in 1957 as 'The Yangtze Incident' and starred Richard Todd.

It was Dr Beeching rather than Hermann Goering who indirectly orchestrated the razing of Victoria Railway Station. The recommendations of the former's reports on streamlining our train services, rather than the bombs of the latter's Luftwaffe, helped remove one of the grandest Victorian sights and sites from the city. In truth, it only just dated from the era of the grand old lady as it opened on 24 May, 1900, about a year after mainline services from London to Sheffield started to pass through. The best quality bricks and Darley stone were used in the construction and the station boasted 12 platforms under a glazed canopy that gave the building a cathedral style effect. Visitors were impressed by the 100 feet high clock tower with its ornate cupola and weather vane. The decline of the railways saw the last passenger train run through here on 3 September, 1966. Historians noted that this was the 27th anniversary of the day that war broke out. The station fully closed a year later and was in the

process of being demolished in 1968 when the photograph of the clock tower amidst the rubble was taken. It is pleasing that the link with the past was preserved, even if it looked a little incongruous amidst the concrete and glass of the Victoria

Above: An aerial view in 1971 of the Victoria Centre flats and shopping centre during construction. The centre and flats were built at the start of the 1970s over the cutting of the old Victoria Railway Station. All that remained of the station was the clock tower on Milton Street. The Centre was to contain high-rise flats, a multi-storey car park, an indoor market (which transferred from the old Central Market opposite The Palais de Danse), a bus station (which had previously been sited on Huntingdon Street), a number of major department stores and Nottingham's flagship branch of Boots the Chemists. It was all enhanced by the whimsical musical clock-fountain by

Centre, as seen in 1973 from Trinity Square and Burton Road, showing the Milton Street entrance. The scaffolding to the right surrounded the Victoria Hotel that was undergoing refurbishment at the time.

Roland Emett, situated just inside the main entrance off Lower Parliament Street. The Centre was officially opened on 16 March, 1973, by Geoffrey Rippon, Secretary of State for the Environment.

These photographs of the Old Market Square illustrate how the face of this part of the city changed in just under three quarters of a century. The more modern image is an aerial view from the summer of 1972. The area, seen during the Nottingham Festival, is much more picturesque, with its landscaped gardens, neatly positioned trees and futuristic centre piece. The city loves such events, holding a variety of them each year in the city centre, on Victoria Embankment, at the Forest Recreation Ground and within the Nottingham Castle walls. In the parade pictured in 1906, the market stalls had all been put away and a large open parade ground left behind. The lines of horse drawn vehicles had assembled as part of the celebrations acknowledging the work done by the RSPCA in its work in caring for the plight of animals. Founded in 1824 by a group of reformers led by Richard Martin MP, the Society came under royal patronage in 1840. A Nottingham branch was founded in 1870 and the current premises can be found on Radford Road.

Hopwells - The Caterer's Choice

A traditional family business with "Fresh ideas for frozen foods", Hopwells Limited is one of the largest family-owned frozen food companies in the UK. Today the business is based in Glaisdale Drive, Bilborough.

The Hopwells story really began on 22nd July, 1944 - the birthday of Timothy Peter Hopwell. He was born in Sandiacre, Nottingham, where he attended Bramcote Hills School. Tim developed a love of trucks from his father; William Hopwell, who ran his own business in Stapleford called 'Universal Demolition Company'.

Tim always worked hard, and when he wasn't out on the truck with his dad he was helping the local milkman do his rounds. After leaving school Tim was given his own milk round. He then left to work for Newark Egg Packers based in Nottingham which regularly brought him to the local markets where he made many friends and became well known by all the market traders, especially the fruit and veg sellers.

Eventually Tim went to work for a firm named R F Willis which had a successful fruit and veg wholesale business with depots at Nottingham, Leicester, Birmingham, Smethwick, Coventry, Kings Cross and Hendon. Tim became one of their many drivers, delivering produce throughout the county. In 1966 he was promoted to Depot Manager at Willis' Meadow Grove site in Nottingham.

However, Tim was both very ambitious and very good at his job. In 1975 he decided to leave R F Willis and set up his own company - T P Hopwell Limited.

*Above: Founder, Timothy Peter Hopwell. **Left:** A young Tim Hopwell climbing on board his father's lorry - where his love of lorries began. **Below:** An old R F Willis (the company Tim worked for and later bought) vehicle dressed for the Victory Parade in 1945.*

here are few of them. "The Company would collect most of the produce on its own transport to get it fresh onto its vehicles for delivery the same day; this meant very early morning starts for those involved in the market operation. One morning we needed to get a pallet of fresh tomatoes back early, so we quickly bought a pallet and despatched it onto our waiting vehicle - a flat-back lorry and sent it on its way to Landmere Lane, Edwalton (Hopwells, first premises). After a few minutes there was a phone call from the driver in a very upset state saying that the full pallet had fallen over and tomatoes were rolling down the hill at the bottom of Hockley (near the market) - needless to say all the waiting vehicles were late out for their deliveries - surprisingly, the driver still works for us today!"

As Tim knew the business so well, and had a great many contacts in the fruit and vegetable trade, the business was soon a huge success. He started the company at Landmere Lane, Edwalton, with just two vans and six staff, but it wasn't long before Tim's good business sense won him the Leicester schools' contract to supply fresh fruit and veg and some frozen food. He needed to expand quickly and purchased another site in Leicester, bought six more lorries and set on another 14 staff.

By all accounts Tim could be a tough task master, but at the same time was always very fair. He worked hard himself and expected the same from his employees - most of whom remain with the company today and who still enjoy exchanging stories about their times with Tim at the helm.

According to Terry Spencer, a now retired long-serving employee and friend of the family: "When Hopwells was in its infancy in the mid-1970s the operation was much different from present day format. There were hardly any frozen foods as it was mainly fresh fruit and vegetables and supplying mainly Local Authority clients. "This meant that the buying operation was achieved by purchasing produce from the Nottingham Fruit & Vegetable Wholesale Market which was then based at Sneinton, Nottingham. The actual buying was mainly done by the late Mr Tim Hopwell and later by Terry Spencer."

Many stories were told of these early morning experiences and

"Most of the stall holders were real characters, like Burt Jacobs who once bought a consignment of new potatoes which were delivered to Nottingham by a goods train, Midland Station Sidings. Because the potatoes were all stacked by hand all our drivers had to pick up their shipment when they had finished their delivery rounds, so that day was a very late day - we never did get to find out why the potatoes hadn't arrived by road. Thank goodness it was before the days of tachographs!"

"Mr Hopwell once employed another buyer who wasn't with us for long. He bought a few tonnes of swede from the market, the problem was that he forgot to tell Mr Hopwell who went absolutely bananas as he had gone and bought several tonnes of

Top left and above: Two views of Tim Hopwell outside the company head office in the early years. *Below:* The growing fleet in the 1980s.

swede himself from another supplier. I think the Local Authorities were fed up of putting swede on the menu for a long time afterwards!"

"After the early morning buying was complete we would go into the market café, which was owned by a lady called Thelma, who was one of the most colourful and outspoken ladies you could wish to meet. It was no good going into her café if you were shy or quiet. She didn't ring a bell when your order was ready; she would shout at the top of her voice in some choice words, everyone would be in stitches - what a character she was."

"There were many more amazing people such as David Hammond, George Smalley, Arthur King, David Russell, Pete Buttery, Malc Pearson, John Heeley to name but a few, some of whom are unfortunately no longer with us. They were at the heart of a busy thriving market which on a daily

basis had some marvellous stories to talk about, not all of which were amusing; some were serious and sad - part of everyday life in an environment that had been in existence for many years in Sneinton."

In 1982 R F Willis, the company Tim had once worked for, was put up for sale. It had previously been taken over by the Imperial Tobacco Group which had in turn then sold it on to the Hanson group who were now selling it themselves. Tim took a gamble and bought this business. It was a particularly proud day for Tim to have purchased the firm which had once employed him.

The firm had depots in Birmingham, Coventry and Daleside Road, in Nottingham. Tim closed the Coventry depot, amalgamated his depot at Landmere Lane and the newly-acquired depot at Daleside Road and bought the premises on Glaisdale Drive, Bilborough, which today is the Hopwells' Head Office.

Hopwells now had a fleet of 80 lorries and employed over 80 staff. In 1986 Tim closed the Leicester Depot and moved to Swadlincote in Derbyshire, changing the name of that depot to

Top and above left: *Hopwells' Glaisdale Drive, Nottingham, head office premises in 1991 (large view) and 1995.* ***Below:*** *The Company's Ormskirk depot pictured in 1996.*

Fresh-Way (Midlands) Limited. The other depots now were only involved in the distribution of frozen foods with all the fresh produce being processed by Fresh-Way.

The business went from strength to strength. In 1991 Tim bought another depot in Sawston, Cambridgeshire, relocating it to a site in Kimbolton in 1993.

In 1994 a Sheffield depot was purchased where a brand new cold store was built three years later. Another depot was bought in Ormskirk, near Liverpool, in July 1996, but sadly Tim died on 9 August, 1996, just three weeks after the purchase. A sixth depot was purchased by the company in 2006 in Darlington, Co. Durham.

Today the company is owned and managed by Tim's wife, Company Chairlady Lilian Hopwell; their son, Tristan Hopwell is the Managing Director. The company now has six depots, a fleet of 100 lorries, over 35 company cars and more than 250 employees.

Hopwells' lorries are a distinctive colour of red and not the usual white that is commonly used within the industry and every Hopwell's lorry has the slogan of 'Success Built on Service' painted on its side - this was the ethos of Tim Hopwell. He believed, and has been proven right, that the success of a business is built on the service it gives.

Hopwells Limited has become a huge success story. The business was truly built on the quality of service it offers to all of its customers throughout their distribution areas. Hopwells is a long-serving member of the British Frozen Food Federation: Hopwells' Operations Director, Phil Holman, sits on the Federation's committee, helping to decide future policies for the frozen food industry.

Each depot has been CMi accredited to the highest level; frozen food is sold to all spheres of the catering industry, including schools, hospitals, social services and to the private sector such

Top and above left: The grand opening of the new cold store at the Hopwells Sheffield depot in 1997 by Mr Alf Carr, Director General of the British Frozen Food Federation, and Mrs Lilian Hopwell, Chairlady of Hopwells. Left: Hopwells Kimbolton, Cambridge. Above: Hopwells' Darlington depot, opened in 2006.

as hotels, pubs, restaurants and cafés. The Company has a strong sales force of professional account managers, experienced and dedicated telesales teams, drivers and cold store operatives working out of each of the six depots to ensure total customer satisfaction at all times.

In 2006 the Company bought its own vehicle repair and maintenance garage on Furnace Road, Ilkeston, Derbyshire, to service and maintain its fleet of 100 refrigerated vehicles. The garage – Total Independent Maintenance - is named t.i.m. Commercial Vehicle Services and employs eight qualified mechanics and four office staff alongside the company's Fleet Manager, Dave Williams. Lilian Hopwell is also based down at the Furnace Road premises where she is most days, other than when she is out and about visiting the other depots in the group.

Tim Hopwell had a vision of a company run on good old-fashioned family values and loyalty, and that tradition is upheld today throughout the Hopwell Group, not least amongst its directors.

Chairlady Lilian Hopwell became an active member of the Board of Directors immediately after Tim's death in 1996. Prior to her role towards making Hopwells the success story it is today, she was kept very busy supporting her husband and raising their two younger children, Ashley and Rosheen Hopwell. She attended many business events standing by Tim's side and went to exhibitions both in the UK and overseas and was, therefore, well known throughout the food industry before becoming the Chairlady of the Hopwell Group.

Outside the business, Tim Hopwell was, and his family still is today, passionate supporters of their home town football team, Nottingham Forest. Tim was very proud of his team and took great pride in sponsoring their youth team and seeing the Hopwells name on their strip. The Hopwell family still are season ticket holders, and other than holiday commitments never miss a home game at the City Ground.

Managing Director Tristan Hopwell joined the family business at the age of 22. He came from the motor industry having served his apprenticeship as a mechanic with Speeds Motor Group and went on to become a sales representative selling new and used Volvos. Tristan was fast-tracked through the different operations of the business due to his father's health problems. Sadly, due to Tim's premature death, they never did get to work together side-by-side.

David Plester, Hopwells' Financial Director, came to Hopwells when Tim Hopwell bought R F Willis in 1982. David was then R F Willis' Accounts Office Manager based at the Birmingham Depot. In 1983 David became the Depot Manager at the Brownhills Depot and then went on to be responsible for the ordering of stock. By 1988 David also managed the company's accounts and was made the Financial Director in 1989, where he remains today.

Andy Breffit joined the company in January 1997 as Commercial Director. He came from Grimsby-based Bluecrest Foods, where he held the position of Director of Foodservice and Hopwells was one of their

Top left: Lilian Hopwell, Tim Hopwell and Tristan Hopwell receiving awards from the British Frozen Food Federation for quality. *Above:* Father and son, Tim and Tristan Hopwell taking great pride in seeing the Hopwells name on the Nottingham Forest strip. *Left:* Hopwells' distribution map.

customers. Andy had been an associate and friend of Tim Hopwell prior to Tim's death.

Operations Director Phil Holman came on board as Operations Manager in 1992. He came from an operational background working with Rowntree Distribution Ltd, followed by a short spell with TDG managing a Sainsbury's distribution site. Phil was made a Director of Hopwells in 1996.

Other long-serving staff include Terry Spencer - retired Depot Manager; Ann Bradley - retired, but longest serving telesales operator; and Terry Herrick, who still works as a multi-drop delivery driver at the Nottingham Depot and Graham Putnam, who has been with the Company from the beginning and is now the Depot Services Manager.

In 2005 Hopwells celebrated 30 years of being in business. A 'Seventies party' was held at Morley Hayes Golf Club, Derbyshire, where the Directors came in 1970s fancy dress in celebration. Staff, suppliers and business associates were also invited to the party.

Hopwells' slogan, 'Success built on service', sums up how the company has maintained its growth over the years. The importance of providing customers with a friendly, consistently reliable service, backed up by an excellent range of innovative food products at competitive prices cannot be over-stated. Every employee knows that only an excellent level of customer care sustains the company's position in the marketplace.

For the future, Hopwells intends to retain its independent status and to continue its steady growth into both new and existing areas of the country. With its unrivalled experience, distinctive branding and an unbeatable reputation amongst caterers, the company looks forward to the coming years with complete confidence in Tim Hopwell's legacy of excellence.

Above: A Hopwells exhibition from the 1990s. Left: The Board of Directors today, (left to right) Tristan Hopwell, Managing Director, Lilian Hopwell, Chairlady, Andy Breffit Commercial Director, David Plester Financial Director and Phil Holman, Operations Director. Below: Company advertising.

ENTERTAINMENT, LEISURE & PASTIMES

Below: This view shows the 'The Empress' pleasure boat in 1905, at its landing stage on the north bank of the River Trent, looking upstream towards Trent Bridge. The steamer was lost at Dunkirk in 1940 (when many private vessels sailed to rescue soldiers trapped by the advancing Germans.

The River Trent has been an historic highway as far back as the Bronze Age when it formed part of the trade route between the Continent and the metal-working industry in Ireland. The Romans recognised the value of the river as a route from the sea to the centre of England.

Above and below: The last freeze over of the Trent occurred in January 1895. For 10 days the river was frozen solid and was deemed to be safe for enthusiastic skaters, so much so that a hockey match was held between Newark and Burton-on-Trent, near to Averham Weirs. Here people, mainly boys, are walking and skating on the ice near to Trent Bridge, looking towards Lady Bay Bridge on the West Bridgford side of the river. Who would have guessed that almost 90 years later Nottingham's own Jayne Torvill and Christopher Dean would be crowned as Olympic Gold Medallists for their dance to Ravel's Bolero, in Sarajevo. They first got together as teenagers in 1975 and used to train regularly after work from 11pm until the early hours of the morning. This dedication paid off as our very own, figure skating superstars went on to become British, European, Olympic and World Champions.

The statue outside the Theatre Royal is of Samuel Morley who was the youngest son of a manufacturer with premises in Nottingham and a warehouse and offices in London. Born in 1809 in Homerton, at an early age he worked for his father's business in London. When his father and brothers chose to retire,

he was left in managerial control. By 1860 he was sole owner of both the London and Nottingham parts of the business, and as it grew rapidly into the largest of its kind in the world he became very wealthy, and a model employer. As a Liberal, he was one of Gladstone's keen supporters, and was elected as an MP for Nottingham in 1865, and later Bristol (1868-85), declining a peerage on his retirement.

Above: Princess Anne unveiling a plaque to commemorate the re-opening of the Theatre Royal on 6 June, 1978. Over 200 years ago, the Theatre Royal was envisaged by two Nottingham lace dressers, William and John Lambert, as a 'temple of drama'...a place of 'innocent recreation and of moral and intellectual culture'. In 1865, the new Theatre Royal was completed. It took just six months to build at a cost of £15,000. It was the work of C.J Phipps, a 29 year old architect who went on to become one of Victorian Britain's leading theatre designers. The Classical facade and Corinthian columns still dominate Nottingham's city centre skyline. One of the most luxurious theatres of its day, the Theatre Royal provided opulent surroundings for the boom of music hall and variety, the birth of light opera, exciting new drama, touring opera and, by the twenties and thirties, the best Hollywood-style musicals and pantomimes. On October 6, 1952, the theatre made history with the world premiere of The Mousetrap (as part of a pre-West End tour). At the theatre that day was writer Agatha Christie along with Richard Attenborough and his later-to-be-wife Sheila Sim, who starred alongside him in the original production. The play has gone on to be the longest running theatrical production in the world. In 1969, the city council bought the theatre and set about restoring it to its former glory. In 1978 the Theatre Royal reopened, boasting elegant foyers and bars, a 1,186-seat auditorium beautifully restored in Victorian style with green and gilt decor. The Theatre Royal is now regarded as one of the best touring venues in the country, attracting major dramas, opera, ballet, West End musicals and, of course, an annual pantomime.

Below: The University's Lakeside Arts Centre that opened in 1992 now sits where Highfields Lido once provided great outdoor entertainment. In 1932, the 44th Nottingham (Leenside) Company of Girl Guides abandoned their uniforms and donned costumes and bathing caps for an afternoon's frolic. Their mothers envied them their freedom because they had been brought up in late Victorian times when even displaying an ankle was considered risqué. Such modesty was a nonsense to these girls. They were part of a new breed of women who could vote, play energetic sports and take on jobs that men traditionally did. The Lido and surrounding grounds were gifted to the people of Nottingham by the pharmaceutical baron, Jesse Boot. He sold his company to an American interest in 1920 and indulged in a flurry of benevolent grants and gifts.

Right and bottom right: This is a view looking south, down the length of the Highfields Lido a year after it had opened in 1924. The open-air swimming pool was 330ft long and 75ft wide and was said to be the largest of its kind in the country. The children could use one of the 250 cubicles surrounding the pool to get changed. Many had walked for miles just to spend a few hours at the Lido. A sundeck was built across the width of the pool in the 1930s. As can be seen from the second photograph, besides providing extra sunbathing

space, the sundeck created a 'small' pool at the shallow end for youngsters. Unfortunately, it also interfered with the proper filtration of the pool and was exceedingly difficult to keep clean. After the Second World War there was a proposal to replace the sundeck with a more open structure that would allow both water and swimmers to pass from one side to the other. In the early 1950s the sundeck was indeed removed but nothing was put in its place and so the pool resumed its original shape. The Lido closed during the 1981 season because it was losing money.

Below: Originally called Bulwell Hall School, by the early 1940s it was known as Springfield School, comprising of a nursery, infants and juniors.. This 1931 picture will be an eye opener to many of our younger readers, as the view shows an open air classroom. Based on open-air principles, this school is one of many built in Nottingham around the 1920s-30s. The open-air movement was taken up by many progressive thinkers in children's education. This followed an international meeting in 1922 of like minded individuals who wished to apply ideas about sunshine and fresh-air and its benefits upon physical and mental health, particularly in the development of children. Many schools were built in support of these ideas. Classes were sometimes run outside in the fresh air or, more usually, inside classrooms with lots of open doors and windows to help pupils with breathing difficulties (caused by such diseases as Tuberculosis and Diphtheria) and to prevent the spread of diseases and infections. It was also partially based on the belief in the association between purity of air and purity of spirit, which it was hoped would lead to happier, healthier children.

Right: Harold Larwood and Bill Voce with their families and friends before setting out on the tour that would become known as the never-to-be-forgotten 'Bodyline' Test series of 1932-33. Harold

Larwood's life in particular, embodied drama given to few cricketers, one of the rare fast bowlers in the game's long history to spread terror in opposition ranks by the mere mention of his name. He was born in Nuncargate, Notts, on 14 Nov, 1904. Larwood left school at 13 and worked in a shop before becoming a pit-boy, working with the ponies. The teenage fast bowler showed distinct promise in  village and junior league matches, and at 19 he was signed by Nottinghamshire. Although only 5ft 8ins, he was strongly-built with long arms and a high arm action. His speed was truly exceptional, and because of his lack of height, his bouncer tended to skid, veering into the ribs rather than wastefully over the head. After his illustrious but somewhat controversial career, shaped by the 1932 'Bodyline' series, Larwood became a post-war migrant welcomed to Sydney in 1950 with his wife Lois and their five children. Bill Voce's name is often associated with his more illustrious partner Larwood, as one of the greatest bowling partnerships. Voce was born in Annesley Woodhouse in 1909 and like Larwood started his working life down the mines. Somewhat surprisingly, he started his playing career at Notts as a slow  left arm bowler. A few years later he added pace to his bowling and although he was somewhat slower than Larwood, his line, from left-arm over the wicket, and the steeper bounce that he obtained from his height, made him formidable enough and the batsmen got no relief when facing him.

Above: At first glance the reader would be excused for thinking that he had stumbled on a photograph from 1922. Was this perhaps Howard Carter uncovering the tomb of Tutankhamen in the Valley of the Kings? On closer inspection, we can determine that the image comes from much closer to home. Mr IJ O'Dell is the man leaning on the shovel. He was one of the members of the Thoroton Society excavating the caves and well under 58 Castle Gate on 15 March, 1939. The group was formed in 1897 and was named after the man who published the first history of the county in 1677. The society has long been the most prestigious of those in Nottinghamshire that are involved in historical and archaeological research. Caves, both natural and man made, are dotted all over the area. Apparently, one ancient name for the district was 'Tiuogobauc'. This translates as 'cave dwellings'. Some of the caves once had windows fixed in place and were obviously used for habitation. Others provided cold storage locations or functioned as small breweries. During the last war, some of the caves acted as air raid shelters, though only those with strong nerves availed themselves of such protection. The more twitchy type of resident preferred a cellar or Anderson shelter. Although the city has lost its medieval buildings above at street level, there is still an underground link with those times. Visitors can look round them as they are now a tourist attraction.

Left: This 1937 view of Sneinton Market, shows Gedling Street and the Town Mission Ragged School building in the background. Sneinton Market is an open air market in the British tradition; it is situated at the western end of Sneinton, where the district meets the city proper and next to the Nottingham Arena. Sneinton market has always sold a strange variety of goods. At the time of this photograph, it sold mainly second-hand articles, from clothing, reading glasses and shoes to bric-a-brac, as well as household goods. Sneinton Market was established around 1850 and there is still a very lively traditional market held every Monday and Saturday. The idea of ragged schools was developed by John Pounds, a Portsmouth shoemaker. In 1818 Pounds began teaching poor children without charging fees. Lord Shaftesbury formed the Ragged School Union in 1844 and over the next eight years over 200 free schools for poor children were established in Britain.

Above: Here in this picture from 1953, a group of almost 40 children from Collygate Infants School, posing proudly in their costumes for the latest pageant. They are probably dressed up to celebrate St George's Day, which is celebrated annually on 23rd April. St. George is the patron saint of England. His emblem, a red cross on a white background, is the flag of England, and part of the British flag. St George's emblem was adopted by Richard The Lion Heart and brought to England in the 12th century. The king's soldiers wore it on their tunics to avoid confusion in battle. The boys in this picture are clearly ready to slay the dragon and rescue the damsel in distress. Collygate Infants School was opened in 1899 in the adjoining building to Mundella Secondary School. At the time of this photograph some readers may remember the brick built air-raid shelter which dominated the playground. In the mid 1980's the school building was taken over by Mundella as a sixth form block and library.

Left: The Forest cheerleaders had plenty to keep them smiling at Wembley on 2 May, 1959. Decked out in the team colours right down to different coloured socks, their team was playing Luton Town in the FA Cup Final. The lads got off to the best possible start, racing to a 2-0 lead within the opening quarter of an hour. But the Wembley hoodoo that had, in recent years, seen several finals hit by injuries to players such as Barnes, Bell, Meadows, Trautmann and Wood, was to strike again. Roy Dwight (1933-2002) had scored the first goal, but after half an hour he went into a tackle and broke his leg. There were no substitutes in those days, so Forest played on with 10 men. After Dwight was stretchered off, Luton became more of a threat. The southerners scored midway through the second half, but our boys held on to win 2-1 and lift the FA Cup for just the second time in the history of the club. Forest returned to the twin towers in 1991, but lost to Spurs. Dwight, as well as being a quiz question on the soccer front, has also appeared as an answer in pop music trivia. The musician, Sir Elton John, is his cousin.

Below: At the time this picture was taken in 1968, Notts County was a struggling side, however, some level of salvation was just around the corner. The Meadow Lane club lurched from one financial crisis to the next and the team was hard pressed to avoid finishing at the bottom of the League and having to apply for re-election. It was a far cry from the heady days when the club shocked the footballing world by signing England centre forward Tommy Lawton from Chelsea. The terraces had gaps where spectators once stood shoulder to shoulder. Diehards still came along every Saturday to cheer on the lads, but often left the ground shaking their heads and longing for the days when they and not Forest were top dogs. In 1969, the club appointed Jimmy Sirrel as its manager. He helped transform County's fortunes, turning it from a struggling Fourth Division side to one that held its own in Division Two. After a spell at Sheffield United, Sirrel returned to Meadow Lane and remarkably piloted the club into the top flight in 1981. Against all the odds, County spent three seasons rubbing shoulders with Manchester United, Liverpool and the rest.

Victoria Embankment is a popular place for a stroll on a warm summer's day. The lapping waters of the Trent make a pleasing background sound that is soothing and relaxing. On this October day in 1974, the river hosted a rally for the Nottingham branch of the Inland Waterways Association. Some 600 narrow boats and river launches turned up to celebrate a pastime that was also a way of life for some. As well as enjoying a relaxing time pottering along rivers and canals, battling with locks and swing bridges, the enthusiasts also provide a useful restoration service. Around two centuries ago, the canal system was developing rapidly. It provided links between both our industrial and agricultural centres and the markets in towns and overseas, via the ports. Raw materials were brought one way and finished products carried the other. The railway era saw the decline of these waterways and, by the start of the last century, many had fallen into disuse. In recent times, volunteers have helped restore some of them to former glories for the benefit of all of us. Even if we do not participate in sailing on the canals or rivers, we can still enjoy ambling along neatly tended banks and towpaths alongside waters that have been cleared of debris. The 1974 rally was held to promote interest in a restoration project being undertaken on Grantham Canal.

Above: Race meetings were originally held on the Forest recreation ground. The races were moved to a new course at Colwick Park and by 1894 the Forest was being re-designed to make it more suitable for other types of recreation, the old stand there was demolished in 1912. Colwick Park was once part of the land attached to Colwick Hall, home to the Musters Family.

Below: The Nottingham Racecourse is set in the beautiful Colwick Park, which is just a short trip from the centre of Nottingham. Although horse racing in Nottingham dates back as far as 1689, the first meeting at Colwick Park took place in 1892 and continued to thrive under the management of the Colwick Racing and Sporting Company until 1965. At this time the 293-acre park was purchased by the City Council for £5 million. Nottingham Races is now known for Flat racing, but in December, 1971, history over the jumps was being made when Stan Mellor steered Ouzo to victory in the Christmas Spirit Novice Chase, to become the first jump jockey to ride 1000 winners. The 34-year-old former champion, had waited exactly a week for the most exciting success of his career spanning 20 seasons. Mellor's wife, Elaine, who had travelled to the races with him every day so as not to miss the celebrations, presented him with an inscribed silver salver (right) on behalf of the Nottingham executive. Who could possibly have thought that 38 years later that total would have been trebled by jumps legend Tony McCoy?

Above: Clifton Market, Southchurch Drive, opened in 1981, and is ideally located on the main shopping street in Clifton. Being well served by local public transport and road links the area is a focal point for the surrounding communities. There are approximately 40 stalls selling a wide assortment of goods, including every kind of fresh produce, crafts, clothing and everyday essentials. Billy Dainty, a British comedian and pantomime star from the 1950s-1980s, is seen here helping out on a stall with Derek and Sheila Roberts, shortly after the market opened. He starred in his own television show in the 1970s and began to appear in pantomime as a dame using his eccentric dancing skills and a funny walk. His television career continued and he became a regular on children's TV in 'Emu's Broadcasting Company' with Rod Hull. In 1981, he was Widow Twankey at the Theatre Royal in Nottingham. This pantomime broke all previous records, generating two and a half million pounds at the box office! It was so popular that the finishing date was extended until it finally ended on April 10, having run into Easter. So successful was it that Aladdin in Nottingham entered the Guinness Book Of Records that year. Billy Dainty was back at Nottingham in 1985 in 'Aladdin' but had to leave due to ill health.

Right: The dome of the Council House contains 'Little John', the striking bell that is probably the deepest toned in the country. The golden ball on top of the dome stands 200 feet above Old Market Square. On 19 December, 1983, the Christmas Fair was in full swing. Sideshows, stalls and a big wheel were all there to provide entertainment, with the usual posse of carol singers ever ready to burst into song. They did not include the current best seller, 'Only You' by the Flying Pickets, in their repertoire. They might have done in other circumstances as this version of a former Yazoo hit was sung in a distinctive capella style, without any instrumental accompaniment. The fair gave way to craft stalls in later years and, in more recent times, there has been an ice rink based in the square and a German Market held here. A glass of Glühwein may not be quite the traditional tipple, but it certainly hits the spot on a chilly evening. Those of us with children in tow will be quite happy to do just what families have done for generations at this time of year. We will go and find Father Christmas somewhere so that the little ones can enjoy a bit of traditional magic. Some of the more observant kiddies will spot that he has shrunk nine inches, lost three stone in weight and developed a lisp since his visit to their school the other day, but that is just one of the oddities of the festive season.

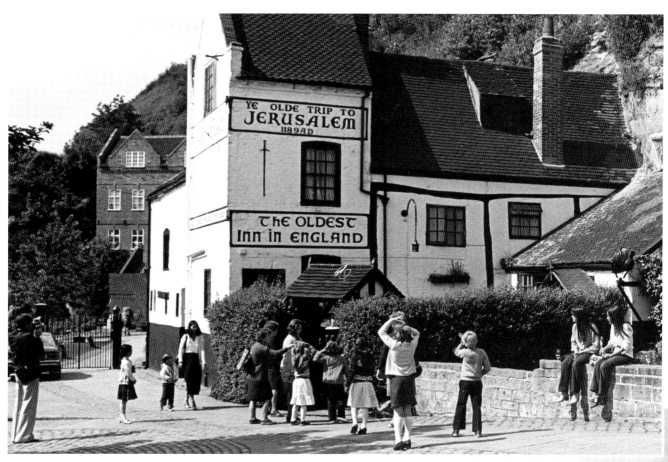

Above: The Trip to Jerusalem pub has a long and venerable history which, as can be seen by the date on its outside wall, goes back to 1189. The Trip claims to be the oldest inn in the world. The one notable thing about 1189 is that it is the date of King Richard I's accession to the throne and this is where the legend begins. We are told the Trip to Jerusalem is so called because the Crusaders, if not Lion-hearted Richard himself, stopped there on the way to the Holy lands on the Crusades to fight the Saracens. The word 'trip' does not necessarily mean a journey in this case. An old meaning for trip is a 'stop on a journey', so the inn's name could mean a stop or rest on the way to Jerusalem. The Trip was also formerly named 'The Pilgrim'. There is evidence that the Castle Rock's caves were in use after the castle was built. It is possible that the caves were being used as the castle's brewhouse in the twelfth century, using a steady supply of water from the River Leen at the bottom of the rock.

Right: It is hard to imagine a more idyllic scene than this at Newstead Abbey. You can almost hear these two chaps singing the Bing Crosby and Louis Armstrongs lyrics 'Gone Fishin', a song written in 1951. Looking across the lake, behind the fishermen, we see one of the two follies built in Newstead Wood on either side the lake by the 5th Lord Byron, in 1749. In view is the stable block complete with bell tower and fronted by the Mock Fort. It is suggested that Lord Byron built the Follies so that he could fight mock naval battles with a miniature fleet of ships. He also erected Folly Castle on a hill overlooking the lake, but this has now been demolished. Historic Newstead Abbey was the Byron family home from 1540, when Sir John Byron acquired it from Henry VIII. George Gordon Byron (the poet) was born in a London boarding house on 22 January, 1788. He was the only child of Captain John Byron by his second wife, the Scottish heiress Catherine Gordon. At the age of ten he became the 6th Baron Byron of Rochdale, inheriting his title and the Newstead estate from his great-uncle William, the so-called 'Wicked' Lord. The poet lived at Newstead for only six years until 1814, when he moved to Italy. Financial problems meant he had to sell the estate but finding a buyer proved difficult. Byron eventually sold Newstead to Thomas Wildman in about 1817, ending nearly four centuries of the Byron family's ownership of the house. After changing hands several times the Abbey was sold to the Nottinghamshire philanthropist Sir Julien Cahn, who presented it to Nottingham Corporation in 1931. Many people who visit Newstead nowadays are eager to learn more about the poet with the racy reputation.

Left: This is the very recognisable Bell Inn, a 15th century Grade II listed building masked by a Georgian frontage, situated on Angel Row off the Old Market Square. Along with Ye Olde Trip to Jerusalem and Ye Olde Salutation Inn it claims to be the oldest in Nottingham. The Bell originally served as a refectory of the Carmelite monastery then sited on Beastmarket Hill, just below St James Street junction. Henry VIII closed small monasteries in 1536 and it then became a secular alehouse, taking its name from the Angelus bell (Latin word meaning 'the noon-day bell') that hung outside. In January, 2002 the pub was purchased by Hardys and Hansons from the Jackson family of Nottingham, who had owned the pub for the previous 103 years. On Trafalgar Day, 21 October, 1898, Joseph Jackson bought the Bell Inn for £12,500 moving from an off-licence in Polin Street, Radford. Mary Jackson succeeded her husband as proprietor in 1913 and established the locally renowned one shilling Market Dinners (vegetable, stilton cheese and a pint of Nottingham ale). In 1998 the Bell was featured along with its rivals Ye Olde Trip to Jerusalem Inn and Ye Olde Salutation Inn in an episode of the Channel TV series History Hunters, to try and determine which was truly the oldest. The inn is now owned by the Green King estate.

SPECIAL EVENTS

Left: This is a view of Avenue E inside the Central Market in King Edward Street during Coronation Week in 1937. The Central Market was opened on 21 November, 1928. It was relocated from the Market Square when the Council House was built. The Central Market again relocated to Victoria Centre in the mid 1970's, and was sadly missed by Nottingham shoppers. A modern brick two-storey development now stands in its place.

Above: The entrance of the Central Market in June 1953 with Glasshouse Street on the left hand side. Window boxes, flags, a large portrait of the new queen, and the royal crest are all clues to the origin of the picture and the reason it was taken; traders here were as keen as others to display their support for the new monarch. The market had been located at this spot since 1928, having been displaced from the original location on the square in front of the Council House. For a period of 44 years the market thrived at its King Edward Street home until it was moved to the Victoria Centre in 1972. There is nothing quite like the atmosphere of a bustling market. Most of us will have childhood memories of visits to the Central Market with our mothers at some time or other, and of the distinctive calls from the traders and the fresh, brightly-coloured produce at the various stalls. On the way out we were treated to an ice-cream at the shop just outside the entrance.

Right: Who would have imagined that a that a lace warehouse assistant from Nottingham would have founded one of the world's greatest football clubs. Yes it's true, Herbert Kilpin left Nottingham for Italy in 1891 where he became one of the charter members and a player of Internationale Torino. Infact, he became the first-ever Englishman to play football abroad. In 1898 he moved to Milan and just a year later he brought AC Milan into existence. Kilpin became Milan's first coach and captain, as well as the team's star player. With Kilpin at its heart the football team won their first league title in only their second season (1901). Kilpin was born in Nottingham on 28 January, 1870, and grew up with nine siblings at 129 Mansfield Road. He was a keen footballer and played in defence and midfield for Notts Olympic and then for St. Andrews, a church team based near the Forest Recreation Ground. Amusingly, according to John Foot in his book 'Calcio, A History of Italian Football', Kilpin was famed for his drinking. He even kept a bottle of whisky in a hole behind the goal. Kilpin claimed this was to soften the blow when the opposition scored. Despite his love of a drink, Kilpin led Milan to a further two championships in 1906 and 1907. He ended his career with Milan when non-Italian players were banned from the league. When World War I broke out he remained in Italy, where he died aged 46. He was buried anonymously in the main cemetery in Milan, in the wing reserved for Christians Protestants. His tomb was abandoned for decades until it was rediscovered by a historian. Appropriately, in 1999, thanks to the interest of the company via Turati, his tomb was moved into a dovecote to the Monumental Cemetery in Milan.

Below: On 8 May, 1945, nearly six years of hostilities in Europe came to an end. The joy on the streets was unbridled and, within a short space of time, impromptu parties were held and parades organised. The ladies' section of the British Legion, Staveley, marched proudly along Chesterfield Road. The flag bearer carried the colours proudly as they honoured those who had served, both at home and abroad, in the defence of freedom. Some of the women fought back a tear, knowing that their husbands and sons would not be coming back, but they shared in the happiness felt by the nation that right had triumphed over evil. The British Legion was founded in 1921 to give social and financial assistance where needed to those who had fought in the Great War and to their dependants. The organisation has been active in promoting the welfare and well being of ex-servicemen ever since.

Above and right: Nottingham Goose Fair dates back some seven centuries, though it was only first mentioned in official records in 1541. It became one of Europe's largest and most important fairs. Until 1876, it lasted for eight days each October, but was then reduced to just five. It had traditionally been based in the Old Market Square, but grew and spread into neighbouring streets, leading to disruption and congestion in the city centre. In 1928, it moved to the Forest Recreation Ground. As can be seen from the 1950 photograph, there were enough sideshows and rides to keep thousands of visitors happy. Helter skelters, dodgems, a big wheel and waltzers offered loads of fun. Bearded ladies, strong men and midgets provided novelties for people to gawp at. There was a boxing booth where foolhardy young men tried it on with grizzled and battle hardened old pros. Quite how good a dart player 'Spot the dog' was in the picture from 1970, is not recorded. He had obviously lost 100 other pals. Since the prizes on offer for accurate throwing included pop records, perhaps he was interested in winning an old copy of 'How much is that doggy in the window?' He could have returned at a later date to get 'Who let the dogs out?'

Above: Cliff Richard once had a hit song called 'When the girl in your arms is the girl in your heart'. Quite right, too. Thank goodness for 'Strictly Come Dancing'! Acting as a reminder to the youth of today that pleasure can be found in the traditional ballroom. Dancing in this fashion was once part and parcel of a normal night out. At the weekend, you had one night on the back row of the pictures and another waltzing and quickstepping away to your heart's content. Being able to fishtail along the floor was a necessary skill and, on more formal occasions, pity the thrusting young executive who trod on the toes of the boss's wife at the office dance. The open air dancing photographed in 1946, was held on the first anniversary of VE Day, when peace was declared to mark the end of the 1939-45 war in Europe. Couples of all ages enjoyed the occasion at the Beauty Spit, Ilkeston, just off Little Hallam Hill. At one time you could enjoy boating and canoeing near here and, in the past, it was a site where carnivals were held.

Bottom left and below: They raided the loft for the bunting and flags that had been in storage since VE and VJ Day. These were strung across roads throughout the nation, just as happened on Basford's Springfield Street, everywhere across the nation. This was 2 June 1953 and it was the day when Queen Elizabeth II was officially crowned as our monarch. She had come to the throne on 6 February 1952, but the country had to wait nearly 16 months for the official period of mourning to end and preparations to be made for the ceremonial coronation. It was an event that had a remarkable spin off in television sales. The goggle box was still in its infancy and few households possessed one, but the BBC had overcome narrow minded resistance from the establishment and had persuaded the powers that be to allow cameras into Westminster Abbey to screen the event. From that day on the importance of radio as the main source of news and entertainment in the home started to decline. Neighbours who had bought a little box with its flickering black and white screen suddenly discovered that they had a host of friends on their street as people crowded into their front rooms to listen to the rich, sonorous tones of Richard Dimbleby describing the events that unfolded before him. In the meantime, children tucked into the goodies mums had baked and got ready to play musical chairs out on the street.

One or two umbrellas had been raised at Wollaton Park in July 1970 as the crowd enjoyed the activities put on as part of the Nottingham Festival. The balloon race had just got under way and the organisers cast an anxious eye aloft. The British weather is notorious for choosing the most inopportune moment to be at its worst. Why does it always seem to rain during a festival, on a Bank Holiday or on the first day of an Ashes Test at Trent Bridge? Despite the vagaries of our climate, we Brits are made of strong stuff and we can still enjoy our high days and holidays, even if they are sometimes a little on the damp side. Still, it was too late to worry as the balloons were off and racing. They filled the skies with colour and the children, in particular, looked at them in wonder.

TRANSPORT

Above: This magnificent example of early 20th century engineering attracted a small crowd of interested spectators. The number plate shows the vehicle to have been one of the first to have been registered. The one or two letter mark at the start of the plate continued until 1932, when an additional letter was added. Registration of road vehicles in Great Britain commenced in 1903 and was operational from January 1904. It was taken outside AR Atkey's garage on Parkinson Street, at the corner with Trent Street. The driver and passenger were well kitted out in order to protect themselves from the elements as Edwardian motoring could be a draughty and damp affair. Of course, such a marvellous machine was a tremendous novelty, so it is hardly surprising that men and small boys quickly came along to gawp. Purchasing such an item of luxury was only for the very well heeled. The age of family motoring for the ordinary man was over half a century away. In the meantime, he could

only admire and feel a little jealous. The owner enjoyed his position of social and mechanical superiority. It was this sort of class divide that would still typify British society for several generations to come.

Right: Driver and conductor posed by the bus bound for South Normanton on the Nottingham route, via Pinxton. Pictured on Wollaton Street in the 1920s, this pair worked in tandem for many years. It would be nearly another half century before one man buses became the norm. They came along from January 1970 and were standard by the end of the decade. Today's young people have missed out on the experience of having a conductor walking the aisle, collecting fares and issuing tickets. He was also in sole charge of ringing the bell to alert the driver, marooned in his cab, when to go or when to stop. Three rings meant that the bus was full and it could sail past a queue of annoyed and frustrated potential passengers waiting at the bus stop. The first motorbuses were introduced in 1906 and were augmented by a fleet of trolleybuses from 1927. As the number of vehicles increased in line with the demand for their services, a new depot was needed. It opened in June 1929 on Parliament Street and continues to be used today. By the mid 1930s the trolleybus numbers had topped 100, making it the largest fleet of such public service vehicles in the country, This number rose even further to 155 by 1952, but the trolleybus era was about to fall into a decline. Not one was left in service by the middle of the next decade.

Right: Trinity Square was the spot where the taxi driver and his passenger posed for the camera in June 1932. The Campion motor cycle and sidecar was manufactured

locally. The Campion Brothers' company was founded in 1901 and was active until 1926. Originally just a bicycle manufacturer, it branched out into motor cycles just before the start of the Great War. Some of its vehicles were fitted with sidecars and used as emergency ambulances at this time. They looked rather strange, but they served a purpose, up to a point as they were not the safest means of transportation. The vehicle seen here was also unusual in being used as one for hire. The passenger in question must have been confident that the heavens would not open, as

the sidecar hood took a few moments to be pulled into place. There was little thought given to such items as crash helmets back in those days. In fact, at the time, road safety was something of a national disgrace. The numbers of injuries and deaths on British roads were, pro rata, among the worst in Europe. We did not even have a simple driving test, so anyone could slip behind the wheel of even the most powerful of vehicles and bowl along the road without so much as a single lesson under his belt.

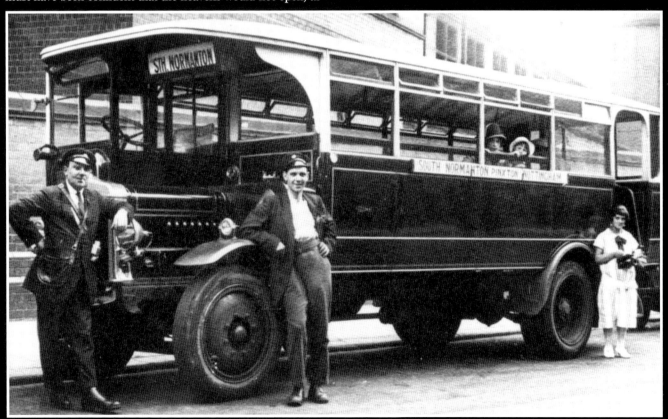

Below: There was a quaint collection of buses, coaches and vans pressed into service as public transport vehicles on Beastmarket Hill, near Market Square. A fire at the Electricity Works at St Ann's Well Road on 17 June, 1925, had put paid to the trams operating. It was to be three days before things got back to normal. Shoppers and office workers were not best pleased having to change their normal routine. Quite how they managed before there were such newfangled modern ideas as electricity was a mystery to those born since the Victorian age. Older locals scoffed at those who complained about the cramped emergency buses and lack of trams. They remembered what is was like when Shanks's pony was the main way of getting from A to B. 'Pampered youngsters!' they snorted, in just the same way we talk about our own youth nearly a century later. Things do not change all that much. The Lyons café on the right was something that also altered little for many decades, though it is sadly with us no more. Joseph Lyons was appointed to run the business that was founded in 1887 as a spin off from the Salmon and Gluckstein tobacco business. The slightly upmarket nature of Lyons' tea shops helped establish outlets on most of our high streets where their interior design suggested that little something extra in taste and decorum. Many of those built during the inter-war years were fine examples of art deco and the uniformed waitresses, nicknamed 'Nippies', were part of the appeal.

Right: Looking NE from King Edward Street, towards the Central Bus Station in March 1932. The Huntingdon Street bus station was first used on 1 January, 1930. Note the early presence of traffic lights at this busy junction. The main bus station re-located into Victoria Centre in the 1970s, and this bus station gradually became unused. The site now houses furniture showrooms and small business units.

Below: We are riding along on the crest of a wave. Well, perhaps not, as this was Cremorne Street and not Mablethorpe. The man at the back, in between the two women, has been identified as Fred Mattison. He was one of a group of residents who took advantage of this novel method of evacuating their homes during the floods of March, 1947. It had been a particularly tough winter, with snowdrifts piled several feet high after the big freeze in February. When the temperatures rose, the inevitable consequence of land and town drains being unable to cope with the volume of water, allied to swollen rivers breaking their banks, meant that we were literally swamped. The cheery smiles on the faces of this group were typical of the British spirit at that time. After all, they had lived through all that Hitler, Goering and crew could hurl at them, so what was a little dampness compared with six years of war?

Above: Author Kenneth Grahame (1859-1932) is best remembered for his 1908 book 'Wind in the Willows'. The driver of this 1933 car might just have been modelled on Mr Toad. It is certainly the type of tourer that would have got the old boy's heart racing, as well as the engine. He would happily speed along the lanes, shouting 'What fun!' and fun it must have been in real life for the owner of such a car. Britain's roads were not cluttered with traffic as they became later on and it was easy to find an open stretch of road and just let rip. This fine example of craftsmanship was first registered in 1933. Younger readers might look at the front of the car and observe a small hole at the bottom of the radiator grille and wonder as to its use. This was where a starting handle was inserted and the engine cranked over if the so called self starting button or interior switch did not succeed in stirring the car into life.

Left: There is something reassuring about the sight of a steam locomotive. It represents strength and security and that all important link with an age when we were top dogs in the world. Loco 45238 had just arrived at London Road Low Level Station on Saturday, 18 May, 1963. It was preparing to accept passengers taking part in a 'Joint Line Railtour'. The route took them to Bottesford, Melton and Nottingham Midland. The outing was organised by the Railway Correspondence and Travel Society (RCTS). It is one of the country's largest societies devoted to the interests of those who love the railways, their operations and histories. Founded in 1928, it flourishes still, organising tours, holding quizzes, hosting events and sales of memorabilia, as well as publishing books and pamphlets. Nicknamed by some as the Royal Corps of Trainspotters, the RCTS is highly regarded by both professionals and enthusiastic amateurs. The Low Level Station was formerly the terminus of the Great Northern Railway. It opened on 3 October, 1857, but was closed passengers on 22 May, 1944. It continued operating a goods service and as a base for occasional passenger specials until 1972. Badly damaged by fire in the 1990s, it was later converted to a health and fitness club. The only steam seen rising then was that coming off weary bodies on the exercise bikes.

Above: How strange it is that half a century and more after this train passed by we should have our rail services grind to a halt because of leaves on the line or the wrong type of snow has fallen. In March 1947, the River Leen was in spate and had broken its banks. Floodwater lapped over the level crossing at the junction of David Lane and Vernon Road. Yet, despite the poor conditions, the steam locomotive and its carriages passed serenely on towards their destination. The waters that poured across the land did so up and down the country, but especially across the lower lying Midlands and East Anglia. The floods were, in the main, attributable to the great thaw that followed the big freeze we had endured that winter. It was one of the worst on record. Heavy snowstorms and sub-zero temperatures combined with a serious fuel shortage, bringing postwar Britain to its knees.

Above: The trolleybus on Lower Parliament Street was one of those vehicles in the Corporation fleet that dominated the city's public transport for 30 years. They superseded the trams, taking over some of their cabling and many of their routes, before passing on the role of transport mainstay to the motorbus. Known in some quarters as 'the whispering death', the first trolleybuses caught some pedestrians unawares. They had become used to the clanking and clanging racket that a tramcar created, warning them of its proximity. Trolleybuses were a different matter. Gliding along very quietly, a careless shopper could step off the pavement without looking and come to a grisly end under a set of very large, unforgiving wheels. The supermarket in view, close to the junction with Newcastle Street, belonged to Fine Fare. This company first traded in Brighton in 1956, before expanding and opening branches in many towns across the country. Seen in 1962, this supermarket was one of the early ones that would later dominate our shopping patterns. Although Marks & Spencer trialled a self service store in Wood Green, North London in 1948, the first supermarket came to Britain in 1950 when Sainsbury's opened one in Croydon. Fine Fare was taken over in 1985 by Somerfield and many of its outlets rebranded as Gateway. The Victoria Centre's new Boots store now occupies this site.

Right: The 1950s drew to a close and the dawn of the swinging 60s was just about with us as we look along Clumber Street, from the junction with High Street, Long Row and Pelham Street. They would prove to be two very different decades. In the former, we continued to suffer the postwar blues for some time. Austerity Britain was a reality for much longer than most pundits had imagined. We even had to suffer partial rationing of some goods right up to 1954, nearly a decade after the last shots were fired. The new spectre on the horizon and threat to peace was the twin thrust of communism and the nuclear bomb. However, with one watchful eye under the bed, looking for Reds, we gradually managed something of an economic turn round. By the end of the decade, ordinary families could just about afford a motor car of their own. There were such former luxuries as electric washing machines, fridges and televisions inside our houses. No wonder that Prime Minister Macmillan announced that we had never had it so good. Despite that, there was something of a revolution in the air and it came with some force in the 1960s. It was change and

AROUND THE SHOPS

not rioting that hit our streets. Led by the young, many old standards of dress, behaviour and attitude were swept away in a tide of optimism. They preached love not war and wanted rid of the old hierarchy. Today, just look across the room and get a glimpse of grumpy old grandpa. He was a frisky firebrand 50 years ago.

The 1965 ceremonial switching on of the lights on the Christmas tree outside the Council House in Old Market Square attracted a crowd that was also entertained by carol singers. Alderman William Derbyshire, the Lord Mayor, officiated. The whole centre twinkled delightfully, setting the tone for a bright and happy festive season. The Council House is a magnificent building and one that reflects the importance of the business conducted inside. It was opened on 22 May, 1929 by the Prince of Wales. He opened the great doors with a golden key that is now on display as a wall plaque near the grand staircase. Local architect TC Howitt's original design was for a shopping centre and office block, but the plans were revised to create new civic premises and chambers. The Council House replaced the old Exchange that had served a similar purpose since 1879. Further back in time, the city had two administrative centres, one for the English community and another one for the French. A Norman building, the Moot Hall, stood at the corner of Wheeler Gate. The English equivalent, the Guildhall, was at Weekday Cross. When the carol singing finished in the square, shoppers hurried off to look for some stocking fillers. Some hummed 'Silent Night', while others preferred to whistle Ken Dodd's 'Tears', a song that outsold any of the Beatles' records that year.

Above: This picture dates from August 1957. It features Chapel Bar, looking west to Derby Road. Until the late eighteenth century this marked Nottingham's western boundary and stretches of the town wall can be seen on Chapel Bar. The Bars were the actual gates in the wall through which traffic would flow from the earliest times of the wall and it is thought likely that these were constructed first. By the sixteenth century these had lost their military purpose and made pleasant walks within the city. In this modern view the shoppers featured were busy with their own concerns.

Above: In this picture from April 1958, British Home Stores can be seen on the left of a busy Lister Gate. Marks & Spencer, one of Britain's favourite retailer, with branches in virtually every town and city of note in the land, is seen facing the camera some 100 yds or so away. In the distance the dome of the Council House and the spire of St. Peter's Church, erected between the thirteenth and fifteenth centuries, can be seen.

Seen from Parliament Street in 1973, shopping on Clumber Street was made much easier once the road had been pedestrianised and cars banned. It had become far too congested, despite the one-way system that had been introduced earlier. The roadway and pavements were not wide enough for either purpose and the city planners created a more shopper friendly area. The faces of town centres all over Britain were undergoing similar changes. New shopping malls were created, linked to multi-storey car parks, and large chain stores took over many of the prime retail outlets. It is obviously a bright but brisk summers day in this late morning scene. The ladies in the picture are clearly not attracted to the prospect of special 'Clynol Wave Curl' hairdo on offer for £2.10 at Continental Hairdressing next to Wigfalls.

This page: The interior of the Broadmarsh Shopping Centre around the time of the opening, showing shops on two floors and a seating area in the centre. The Broadmarsh Centre was opened in March, 1975, by the Duke of Gloucester. Westfield Broadmarsh as it is now known, is the southern end shopping centre in Nottingham. The Broadmarsh Centre was built upon streets which had been cleared of slum yards and housing. Foundations were begun in the late 1960s. Streets such as Drury Hill, which had contained timber framed buildings, disappeared and caves which ran underneath were obscured. Many ancient

caves and cellars dug into the soft sandstone foundations of the city were rediscovered. Pressure from residents and historians allowed the caves to be preserved instead of destroyed, This resulted a popular shopping centre with the public, but with the rather soul-less facade which can be seen here in the early 1970s. Things have improved, however. The centre received a major cosmetic refurbishment in 1988 and the 'City of Caves' exhibit beneath the shopping centre is now a major tourist attraction.

Left: This picture was taken at the official opening of the Time Fountain in 1973. The Time Fountain, situated in the Victoria Centre, is a silver-white coloured four faced clock on top of a moving sculpture. It consists of a large copper flower, whose petals open on striking. It contains a variety of mechanical animals including squirrels, peacocks and fish, playing musical instruments, that turn when the clock strikes. Three arms are extended out, one flying fish, one squirrel and pram and a peacock rowing, as well as lots of little birds. The clock strikes every quarter hour. Rowland Emett, its creator, is quoted as saying, 'it is an aquahorological tintinnabulator.'

Below: A May 1973 view outside the entrance of the Victoria Centre a year after it opened for business.

BIRD'S EYE VIEW

Left: By 1927, when this aerial shot was taken, Notts County was already a 65 year old pensioner. Founded in 1862, it is the world's oldest professional soccer club, Sheffield FC predates it by five years, but that has been primarily an amateur club. Initially, County played at Park Hollow in the grounds of Nottingham Castle, before moving to Trent Bridge. In 1888, the club was one of the 12 inaugural members of the Football League. Of that first dozen, only Accrington FC, not to be confused with Accrington Stanley, no longer exists. Notts County has several other claims to fame, though these all date back many, many years. It won the FA Cup in 1894 as a second division side in a match that saw Jimmy Logan score the first FA Cup Final hat trick. The famous black and white striped strip was copied by no lesser team as the Italian side, the mighty Juventus, who needed a new kit in 1903 and were supplied by a Nottingham clothier. In 1910, County left Trent Bridge and moved to the Meadow Lane ground that has been its home ever since. Its highest attendance of 47.310 was achieved in 1955 for a Round 6 FA Cup tie against York City. That figure will never be beaten as, in the wake of the Bradford City and Hillsborough disasters of the 1980s, the dilapidated stadium was remodelled in the 1990s. Meadow Lane now holds just under 20,000.

Above: A bridge has existed at or around the current location since 924 during the reign of Edward the Elder when an oak superstructure was supported by stone piers - with evidence that the site also had a ferry during occupation by the Danes. The bridge as it appears today was constructed over a three-year period between 1868 and 1871, for the price of £36,000. Construction took place alongside the existing bridge, until the completion of the new bridge allowed the older structure to be demolished. Two of the approach spans to the older bridge still remain, next to the road outside County Hall. The bridge was then widened (1924-6) to allow the six-lane capacity that exists today. Shown on the left of the 1925 picture are the Town Arms public house and Turney's leather works, and on the right the site of County Hall, Pavilion Cinema and Nottingham Forest Football ground (The City Ground).

The bird's eye view of the city centre was taken in March, 1973. It shows the face of modern Nottingham, as opposed to the style of earlier times in the last century. In those days the profile was lower, without the office blocks, multi-storey car parks and flats that rose up during the 1960s. Maid Marian Way was upgraded to an inner-city dual carriageway in 1964. Friar Lane runs from bottom right to centre left. It's an historic route and leads from the castle to the city centre. The intersection with Maid Marian Way was turned into a roundabout with a central pit that linked four pedestrian subways. Although this major road acted as an inner traffic circuit, it also created something of a barrier in separating one section of Nottingham from the other. In the early 1990s consideration was given to sinking the road into a tunnel, but this was rejected on cost grounds. By the start of this century, Maid Marian Way was widely considered to be one of the worst streets in the country. However, a major face lift has latterly restored some of its pride. The creation of wide pedestrian crossings has given both a visual and practical link across this busy road. In addition, large areas of public space have been created with roomy pavements and attractively planted spots. In the photograph, Park Row runs across from centre right, where the General Hospital and its Jubilee and Trent Wings can be seen.

An aerial view of the Trent Bridge area in 1975, showing Trent Bridge and the River Trent at the bottom left of the picture. Trent Bridge Cricket Ground is centre right, with County Hall in the extreme right foreground. Founded in 1841, Trent Bridge is the world's third oldest major cricket ground, preceded by Lords and Eden Gardens, Calcutta. Radcliffe Road is in the centre right. Lady Bay Bridge is top left and the Bridgford Hotel is the bow-fronted building next to Trent Bridge. Loughborough Road goes off to the right and Nottingham Forest Football Club is in the centre showing a stand under construction. This was to coincide the arrival of the man whose name will always be etched in the folklore of Nottingham Forest Football Club. Brian Clough arrived in January of this year and under his colourful and often controversial leadership, Forest would go on to scale unprecedented heights by winning the European Cup in 1979 and 1980. He also took Forest to the record unbeaten run for any League Club at the time, when, between November, 1977, and December, 1978, they went 42 matches undefeated.

A bronze statue of the legendary football manager was unveiled infront of more than 5,000 people in November, 2008. The statue is sited near the Old Market square in Nottingham city centre.

Below: Nottingham High School was founded by Dame Agnes Mellers in 1513 and is therefore almost 500 years old. It has been a place of inspirational learning for a number of public figures in Nottingham, including DH Lawrence and Jesse Boot, founder of the chemist's Boots. The school was originally situated in Stoney Street, but was moved to its present site between the Arboretum and the Forest in 1868. Since then many alterations and additions have been made. Its name was changed from that of the Grammar School to the High School in 1868. The school was probably the first day school in the country to introduce a 'tutorial' system, by which every boy had a master throughout his career in the school, who was responsible of his welfare. The school is now an independent school for boys aged 5-18 and has a proud history and tradition with an excellent academic reputation. This aerial view is from June, 1973, and features the school on Waverley Mount, sandwiched between Forest Road East and Arboretum Street.

Right: The view along Mansfield Road was taken in 1976. Looking north from the junction with Forest Road, it shows St Andrew's Church in the foreground. This place of worship was built in 1871 by William Knight. The nearby cemetery was created under the Nottingham Enclosure Act of 1845 and was designed by Edwin Patchitt. It opened in 1856, but the mortuary chapel was not added until 1879. This building was demolished in 1965. The burial grounds are also known as Rock Cemetery. They are built on old sandpits that were once quarried or mined for sand to be spread on house floors or used as an abrasive cleaning agent. To its immediate northwest we can see the Forest. This recreation ground and public park covers more than five hectares in the area that once formed part of the start of the mighty Sherwood Forest where Robin Hood supposedly robbed the rich for the benefit of the poor. We can also see Clarendon College that, since 1999, has been part of New College, Nottingham, and the former Savoy Hotel.

WORKING LIFE

Below: In 1901, many cities were just like ours. They prepared to usher in the new age of electricity with the biggest revolution in public transport since the railways burst upon the scene in the 1830s. These maintenance workers would be busy men over the next three decades as they kept the tramcars in tip top condition. Piles of wheels, bogeys and lay waiting to be fitted. The Sherwood Depot was situated on Mansfield Road, between Melrose Street

and Daybrook Street. If you happen down that way today, the large doors and the street façade are still in evidence. One of the first tram routes to be used was from Trent Bridge to St Peter's Square, but this used a pair of horses to provide the power. The line from Market Place to Carrington Road saw the first electrically powered cars at the start of 1901. Within a matter of months we had a fleet of 77 open topped trams. The face of the city centre altered dramatically. It was opened up to people in the satellite villages and towns. Beforehand, it had been something of an expedition to leave home and travel several miles into Nottingham. Now, the journey could be accomplished in relative comfort and in a matter of minutes rather than hours.

Above: Nottingham is seen as the metropolis of the lacemaking industry. It is one of the key aspects of the history of Nottingham, and a quarter-mile square area in the heart of the city contains one of the enduring signs of the impact lace has had upon the area. It was officially named "The Lace Market" in 1847. Many of the local Nottingham businesses were focused solely on the finishing of lace which was made elsewhere in the East Midlands countryside. Unfinished lace was often limp, tangled and dirty, and sometimes stained with the very graphite and oil that kept the machines running efficiently. The finishing tasks were performed mainly by women, often in factory surroundings that were overheated, poorly ventilated and poorly lit. Many warehouses in the Nottingham Lace Market were conversions of dwelling houses of the 1700's and working conditions were usually poor. Thomas Adams, a noted Quaker, did much to reform the working conditions for the ladies in his factory, providing indoor toilets, a tea room, daily chapel services and a sick fund. At about the same time, during Queen Victoria's mourning for Prince Albert, a fashion for black lace swept the country. Throughout the early 1900s, Nottingham dominated the machine-made lace industry, with nearly all of the machine lace in the United Kingdom being produced, finished, processed or shipped through one or another of the city's lace businesses. The trade began to decline only in the 1950s, when it became less expensive to establish factories and machines overseas where the labour was cheaper. Cotton lace has been replaced with synthetic and elastic threads, and the vast majority of lace is now used for undergarments, rather than outerwear.

Above: Bestwood Coal and Iron Company's colliery, pictured here in the 1920s, was originally known as The Lancaster Drift after the family who owned the colliery from its beginnings in 1871 to nationalisation in 1947. The drift was a long tunnel which plunged into the earth at a one in four gradient, and brought one million tons of coal a year direct from the High Main Seam to the surface. It was Europe's largest colliery drift. The drift took five years to complete and would have been finished earlier but for difficulties encountered when driving through the water bearing sandstone which was only eighteen meters below the surface. Bestwood's winding engine house and headstocks remain as a monument to the once thriving Bestwood Colliery that closed in 1967 (The ironworks closed in 1928). The building has three stories and is red brick, partially faced in stucco with a hipped Welsh slate roof. Inside the engine house is the steam driven winding engine, which is unique. It is a vertical winding engine and was believed to have been built by Wren and Hopkinson of Manchester. The Science Museum at South Kensington, London, gave a grant for its restoration. It is believed that the Bestwood Colliery fan engine was originally in the steam ship 'Royal Sovereign', which was thought to have sunk in the Mediterranean and the engine salvaged. The Lancaster's, the owners of the colliery, built Bestwood Colliery Village in 1876. The houses were some of the best in the East Midlands. A small front garden was complemented by a walled back garden. The village attracted workers and their families from many parts of the country.

Right: A rare photograph of ladies are pushing their unusual milk churn trolleys for a promotion of the Co-op's service around 1910. The posters on the carts say that they 'deliver twice daily, with an annual distribution netting £35,000'. The ladies would serve the milk using pint and quart measures straight from the churn, and the milk would be supplied by the Co-op's own farm. The spectators dressed in their 'best clothes' suggests that the ladies were part of a parade or event.

Left: The first telephone system, known as an exchange, which is a practical means of communicating between many people who have telephones, was installed in Hartford, Connecticut in 1877, and the first exchange linking two major cities was established between New York and Boston in 1883. The first exchange outside the United States was built in London in 1879 and involved a group of operators working at a large switchboard who would answer an incoming telephone call and connect it manually to the party being called. Manual switchboards remained in common use until the middle of the twentieth century. The women pictured in this 1973 photograph at the Telephone Exchange, in Broad Street, would have been highly delighted just to be in employment. Following the end of World War II, there was a long interval without a major recession (1945 – 1973) and a growth in prosperity in the 1950s and 1960s. However, following the severe shock of the 1973 oil crisis and the 1973–1974 stock market crash, the British economy went into recession in 1974. The lovely lady overseeing at the desk behind looks rather stern faced. This could be a misconception but I think if I had worked there I too would have kept my head down!!

Luxfer - Global and Local

Based in Colwick, on the edge of Nottingham, Luxfer Gas Cylinders has a story that began with 19th-century Victorian entrepreneurship and now spans the globe.

From manufacturing facilities in the United Kingdom, France, the United States, China and India, Luxfer supplies high-performance cylinders to customers around the world. Gas suppliers and users know that the Luxfer brand stands for aluminium and composite products of unsurpassed quality and reliability, even in the most demanding applications.

apparatus (SCBA) for life support, compressed natural gas (CNG) for alternative fuel vehicles, fire extinguishers, beverage, industrial speciality gas, SCUBA, paintball, performance racing and inflation, as well as a line of spun aluminium and steel cylinders for specialised services.

A member of the global Luxfer Group of companies (www.luxfergroup.com), Luxfer Gas Cylinders has grown to be a world leader in the gas-containment industry. With nearly 50 million cylinders in service, Luxfer Gas Cylinders is truly living up to its motto: "Setting the standard worldwide".

Luxfer's diverse product line ranges from small aluminium cylinders that hold four cubic feet (113 litres) of gas to large cylinders standing five feet tall and holding 265 cubic feet (7,504 litres). These all-metal cylinders are made exclusively from alloys developed by Luxfer metallurgists, including L6X®, Luxfer's proprietary version of AA6061, and L7X®, a patented, higher-strength alloy that allows higher-capacity gas filling. Luxfer is also the world leader in hoop-wrapped composite cylinders and ultra-light, full-wrapped carbon composite cylinders used for a variety of applications.

The company manufactures cylinders for a wide range of markets, including medical, self-contained breathing

LUXFER: A BRIEF HISTORY

The Luxfer story began on 17th February, 1885 in Boston, Massachusetts, when British-born inventor and entrepreneur James G. Pennycuick received a USA patent (No. 312290) for prismatic glass tiles. In his patent application, Pennycuick described his product as 'an improvement in window-glass.' His improvement was moulding a series of triangular ridges to one side of a four-inch-square clear glass tile, thus creating prisms that would

Above: *Modern lightweight composite gas cylinders wrapped in carbon fibres.* *Below:* *Luxfer Gas Cylinders, Colwick Industrial Estate, Nottingham.*

extremely well, he had not yet come up with an economical way to bond them together into large windows. That problem was solved several years later when Pennycuick met American inventor William Winslow of Chicago, Illinois. Winslow created an electro-glazing process that used small copper strips and an electrolytic bath to bond Luxfer tiles into strong, rigid window panels. These large panels redirected sunlight from areas where light was plentiful into interior spaces where it was scarce.

Partnering with another American, Thomas W. Horn, Pennycuick founded the Radiating Light

refract sunlight into dark spaces. He named his light-bearing invention "Luxfer"—from the Latin "lux" (light) and "ferre" (to carry or bear).

On 11th August, 1885, Pennycuick was granted yet another USA patent for a "Method of Forming Screw-Threads on Glass." Using this method, he devised a unique design for glass electrical insulators and began organising a company to produce them. In December 1889, Pennycuick purchased a glassworks factory that had closed in 1888. Located on Cape Cod, in Sandwich, Massachusetts, the facility had been owned by the Boston and Sandwich Glass Company, which had once produced some of the finest hand-blown and pressed glassware made in North America.

Pennycuick was eager to get his newly-acquired glassworks, now called the Electrical Glass Corporation, up and running again. Even before his own plant was operational, he had samples of his new insulator made by the nearby Sandwich Co-operative Glass Company. The samples brought in a flood of orders, but Pennycuick quickly ran into major logistical and labour problems with his own factory—so much so that in November 1890, only six months after he began making products, he was forced to cease operations. Lenders soon foreclosed on the factory and sold it at a public auction.

Undaunted, Pennycuick turned back to his first patent for 'Luxfer' light-bearing prism tiles and began working toward starting a new company. But Pennycuick faced another challenge. Although his small prisms refracted light

Above: An Early twentieth century view of a London department store using Luxfer prism tiles. *Right:* Building schematic.

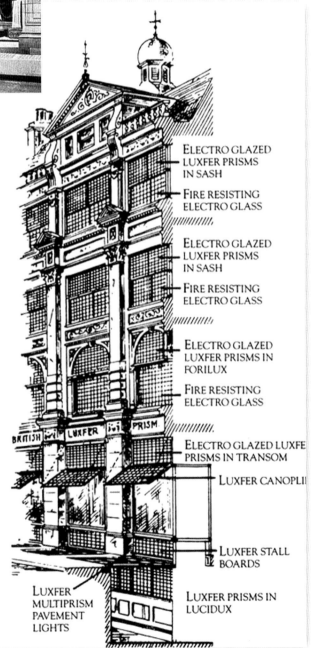

ELECTRO GLAZED LUXFER PRISMS IN SASH

FIRE RESISTING ELECTRO GLASS

ELECTRO GLAZED LUXFER PRISMS IN SASH

FIRE RESISTING ELECTRO GLASS

ELECTRO GLAZED LUXFER PRISMS IN FORILUX

FIRE RESISTING ELECTRO GLASS

ELECTRO GLAZED LUXFER PRISMS IN TRANSOM

LUXFER CANOPLII

LUXFER STALL BOARDS

LUXFER MULTIPRISM PAVEMENT LIGHTS

LUXFER PRISMS IN LUCIDUX

Company in Chicago in October 1886. Two months later, they changed the name to the Semi-prism Glass Company, and finally, in April 1897, they settled on the name the Luxfer Prism Company and began producing tiles at a factory in Chicago.

Pennycuick hired prominent physics professor and spectroscopist Henry Crew of Northwestern University in Chicago and his assistant Olin H. Basquin to optimise the performance of Luxfer prisms. Basquin is credited with being the first scientist to record sky brightness. He used his knowledge to calculate the best angles so that Luxfer prisms would make maximum use of available light.

Pennycuick also hired a 30-year-old American architect named Frank Lloyd Wright to create decorative designs for Luxfer tiles. Although Wright designed 41 patented tile variations, only one—the well-known 'flower' pattern that is now a much-sought-after collector's item—was actually

produced. Wright, who later became the most famous architect in the USA, used Luxfer tiles extensively in his early buildings.

Architects and builders throughout North America began using Luxfer prismatic tiles and windows to illuminate building interiors, as well as basements and tunnels—a process they called 'daylighting'.

In 1898, Pennycuick travelled to London, where he founded a subsidiary company, the British Luxfer Prism Syndicate, established under licence from the American company to make windows as well as glass pavement tiles to illuminate cellars and basements. (Also in 1898, the name of the original company was changed to the American Luxfer Prism Company.) Many Luxfer tiles can still be seen in cities and towns across Britain, especially in the sidewalks of

London. Within five years, Luxfer branched out around the world as more and more architects incorporated Luxfer prisms into their designs.

By 1910, millions of Luxfer glass tiles were being produced each year, and the company had added fireproof window glazing to its product range.

During the First World War (1914-1917), Luxfer's London factory produced the company's first metal products: 'screw picket' posts to support rolls of barbed wire on battlefields. Post-war Luxfer began producing metal fasteners and other construction components.

In the 1920s, the demand for Luxfer glass tiles declined as the use of electric lighting became more widespread. In response to the changing market, Luxfer began manufacturing ready-glazed windows and added new metal products to its range, including sheet-steel shelving, cabinets and office furniture.

During the Second World War (1939-45), Luxfer used its metal-finishing expertise to produce a variety of armaments

Top left: Metal office cabinets. *Above:* Luxfer prism tiles, circa 1900. *Left:* Luxfer France, formally Société Métallurgique de Gerzat (SMG).

and military products capable of withstanding harsh battlefield environments.

In 1945, Luxfer introduced an extrusion process for applying putty to ready-made windows used in prefabricated houses in England that replaced homes damaged during wartime bombing. This new process soon led to a line of extruded metal products, including tubing. By the 1950s, Luxfer tubing products were widely used in cars, aircraft, scaffolding and a variety of home and office equipment, including Hoover vacuum cleaners.

To supply mortar shell casings and rocket bodies for bazookas during the Korean War (1950-1953), Luxfer introduced a new process called cold-indirect extrusion, an engineering milestone that changed the course of the company's history and led to the development of the world's first cold-extruded aluminium gas cylinders.

GAS CYLINDERS: THE EARLY DAYS

The first gas 'cylinders' were animal bladders used in the 18th century to contain gases in laboratories. Later came gas bags made of oiled cloth, as well as silk covered with gilt paint. The first metal cylinders came from Germany in 1886, when Max and Reinhard Mannesmann developed a method for producing seamless steel tubes by extrusion. Their method was soon

adapted to the manufacture of gas cylinders, a significant step in the development of the industrial gas business.

In 1891, Harrisburg Pipe and Pipe Bending Works in Pennsylvania USA received requests for containers to hold anhydrous ammonia gas, the activating agent for making dry ice. The containers needed to withstand temperature changes without cracking. Workmen made a containment cylinder for the gas using a discarded piece of 5-inch-diameter pipe measuring 51 inches in length. Soon after, the company used pipes of the same size to fill an order for 20-pound carbon dioxide cylinders—and those dimensions became the standard for industrial gas cylinders.

For many years, high-pressure gas cylinders were made primarily of steel, making them heavy to lift and use, susceptible to rust and corrosion and expensive to transport.

Then in 1941, a French company called Société Métallurgique de Gerzat (SMG) used hot-extrusion technology to produce the world's first aluminium gas cylinders, which were much lighter in weight than steel cylinders yet capable of holding comparable high gas pressures. (SMG was acquired by Luxfer Gas Cylinders in 2001 and is now called Luxfer France.)

ENTER LUXFER

In 1958, Luxfer introduced the world's first cold-extruded aluminium cylinders, and the company soon opened its factory in the Colwick suburb of Nottingham to produce its unique high-pressure cylinders. Luxfer employs a hydraulic

Top left: Korean War mortar. **Below:** *The new lightweight aluminium cylinders were first used in public houses.*

ram to press and shape a solid aluminium billet into a hollow shell, the open top of which is then closed and threaded. The result is a seamless, lightweight aluminium cylinder with a consistent wall thickness and naturally corrosion-resistant oxide finish that make it ideal for the high-pressure storage of gases.

Lightweight Luxfer aluminium cylinders were initially used to replace heavy, corrosion-prone steel CO_2 beverage cylinders in British public houses. During the 1960s, the company rapidly expanded its product range to include cylinders for many other applications, including industrial gases, medical oxygen, fire extinguishers, life-support for firefighters and rescue personnel, scuba diving and various automotive and aviation uses. Luxfer sold its non-cylinder product lines in 1965 and began concentrating on its rapidly expanding cylinder business.

In the mid-1960s, Luxfer installed what was then the world's largest extrusion press in its Nottingham factory, enabling the company to make larger cylinders and expand into a variety of industrial markets. Today Luxfer makes the largest high-pressure aluminium gas cylinders in the world.

Luxfer opened its first aluminium cylinder manufacturing plant in the USA in Riverside, California, in 1972. In 1976, the company expanded its product range to include higher-pressure hoop-wrapped composite cylinders with fibreglass-reinforced walls. The next major development came in 1986 when Luxfer introduced lightweight composite cylinders fully wrapped with fibreglass (and later Kevlar®). Luxfer opened an aluminium cylinder factory in Graham, North Carolina USA, in 1991.

Above: *The Luxfer Plant in Graham, North Carolina.*
Below: *Luxfer Shanghai, manufacturing composite life-support cylinders.*

As the demand for gas-containment rose in the Far East, Luxfer opened its Luxfer Shanghai factory in 2006 to manufacture composite cylinders for China and the rest of the Asia Pacific market.

The following year Luxfer began manufacturing composite alternative fuel (AF) cylinders in California for use in trucks and buses, as well as for storage and transportation of compressed natural gas (CNG).

Luxfer consolidated all its USA composite cylinder operations under one roof in a state-of-the-art manufacturing facility in Riverside, California, in 2008.

In Northern Italy, Luxfer opened a European Alternative Fuel Centre in 2009 to supply compressed natural gas fuel (CNG) storage systems for buses and trucks. Using CNG helps reduce dependence on oil whilst delivering significant environmental benefits.

Also in 2009, Luxfer and Uttam Air Products, a leading gas manufacturer in India, signed a joint venture agreement to manufacture cylinders in that country.

The spirit of entrepreneurship and innovation that characterised Luxfer's early history is still very much a part of the company's culture today. A number of new products are on the drawing board that will help Luxfer continue 'setting the standard worldwide'. For more information about the company, please visit www.luxfercylinders.com

In 1997, Luxfer introduced even lighter-weight composite cylinders fully wrapped with aerospace-grade carbon composite fibre. Initially used for firefighter life-support, these ultra-lightweight, high-capacity cylinders were soon introduced into other markets, including medical, automotive, aviation and paintball.

Expansion now came through acquisitions. In 1998 Luxfer bought Hydrospin, a California-based manufacturer of seamless aluminium liners for composite cylinders, as well as specialised aluminium and steel cylinders and pressure vessels. Three years later, the company acquired French cylinder manufacturer Société Métallurgique de Gerzat (SMG), which became Luxfer France. Luxfer France added a new full-wrap composite cylinder facility to its Gerzat plant in 2005.

Top left: *High-strength, ultra-lightweight carbon fibre is used to reinforce Luxfer composite cylinders.* ***Left and below:*** *Luxfer lightweight aluminium cylinders have many applications, including their use in fire-fighting and scuba diving.*

Caunton - Engineering the Future

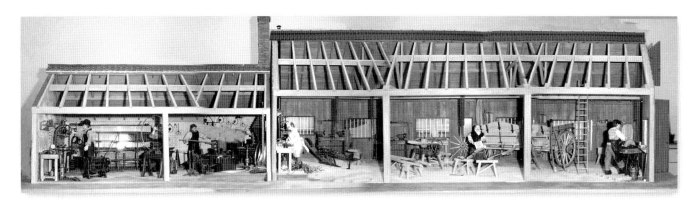

There has been a blacksmith's shop in the village of Caunton, near Newark since records began. Famously Charles I raised his standard in Nottingham. Newark Castle was a royalist stronghold, but after Charles I surrendered in 1646 Oliver Cromwell had the castle dismantled. Cromwell billeted his army just three miles away from Caunton where various services required by an army were available: wheelwright, farrier, sword mending and other metalwork.

In 1822 there were two blacksmiths and a wheelwright's shop in Caunton, but by the time Tom Broadberry bought his business in 1968 there was only one. In 1840 Henry Gilbert had purchased the business and land that the blacksmith's forge was built on. Henry Gilbert built a fire pit next to the beck for heating iron. The beck was diverted into a new quenching pit, providing water to shrink hot iron tyres and lock the wheel segments into place before the wooden wheel could be damaged by the heat.

The Gilbert family bought two cottages on Chapel Lane (then Wood Lane) which came with the forge when Tom Broadberry bought the site. The cottage nearest Main Road became offices - this too had been a blacksmith's shop, worked by Thomas Watson from 1851. The wooden beam over the front of the shop has carved into it J.R.H 1790 – presumed to be the blacksmith back then. There is also a record of a wheelwright, a Mr Ford. The Gilberts also kept cattle in the surrounding fields and had a dairy at the Croft, which in an earlier life had been the 'Fox and Hounds' beerhouse and brewery.

Generations of Duffyns were blacksmiths and wheelwrights too. When the last one, Tom Duffyn, retired he sold his business to Reg Hardwick. Reg took the business into engineering, making steel-framed farm buildings. Eventually Reg sold the business to Tom Broadberry who added specialist welding service for contractors' plant to the services on offer.

Tom built a new crew yard for the Harvey's at Maplebeck in 1969. This was a steel portal frame, and it was this connection, along with the fact that George Brough, the Nottingham motorcycle manufacturer, whose favourite hideout with his girl friends was the Beehive pub in the village, that led to name of Caunton's holding company Maplebeck Holdings.

After eighteen months working on his own Tom had completed over four hundred jobs. His wife Molly tended to the administration and accounting side of the business.

*Top: A model of the Caunton Forge and Wheelright's circa 1900. **Left:** David Bingham and Tom Broadberry, Co-founders of Caunton Engineering Limited. **Below:** Caunton Forge in 1969 when its was turned into a limited company.*

off at the rear and move along with the truck so it could collect spoil from trenches into the lorry. The conveyor was supported on a stand whilst the full lorry was exchanged for an empty one.

In 1969 Tom approached David Bingham to join him in partnership: Caunton Engineering Ltd came into being on December 18th. The business plan was to specialise in contractors' plant and farm machinery. The staff consisted of Tom Broadberry, David Bingham, both former Sir Robert McAlpine employees, and their wives doing the bookwork part time. The first employee was Ed Myers who was off sick for the first week.

On 1st March 1970 Alex and Michael Coulter joined from McAlpine just in time to see the business plan change completely. The company still manufactured and repaired plant, but at the invitation of local farmer, and later M.P. for Newark and Sherwood, Andy Stewart, the business moved into manufacturing farm buildings. The first building was a lean-to on a Dutch barn. Caunton completed the whole job, including foundations, walls, gates and feeding racks. Simon Bingham was born the day after the building was completed on 18th April, 1970. Andy Stewart, being a canny Scott, was highly regarded in the local farming world and the firm soon had orders from the

Top left: Caunton's first job was a piece of handrailing for MFI opposite Midland Station in Nottingham. Other early jobs were rollers and trailers for farmers and Squires Plant. Top right: Co Founder David with family Jill, Simon and Sara in 1970. Left: Caunton's first building was for Andy Stewart. Below: Caunton's first free standing building, a Dutch Barn for Peter Applewhite, Norwell, in 1970.

The company took on all manner of jobs in the early days, anything that would turn a penny. The first job was a piece of fence for MFI in Nottingham; another was a fireplace dog grate for Ken Wagstaff a local builder. It weighed 12.5 lbs and cost £14 14s 2d. making a rate of £2,643 per tonne. This was in February 1970 - a wonderful rate per tonne even today!

Within ten days there was an order for several specialist conveyors from Mike Holmes of Cable Lines Construction. The conveyor needed to be carried by a lorry and then slide

surrounding villages; Jack Todd, John Boddy, Tommy Seal, Peter Applewhite and Mrs. Mary Hole being the first.

Caunton quickly moved into free standing buildings, the cost of which were much more predictable. By the summer the firm had secured a series of contracts from the County Council erecting new farm buildings for its farms in Rolleston, Sutton on Trent and Gamston.

As the firm's reputation spread it was soon working throughout Nottinghamshire, Derbyshire and Lincolnshire and had outgrown Caunton. The company was becoming a nuisance to the local population, leading to frequent visits from Planning Officers. Another home was found in 1972 on Lowmoor Road, Kirkby in Ashfield where a new factory opened at Easter 1973.

The new premises were custom built for structural steel fabrication, with overhead mobile cranes and new plant and equipment. John Deakin joined as general manager and Ray Turton as Works Foreman. Their first job was to design and build the new factory. Ray worked through the winter in Tom's

brother, Bob Broadberry's, farmyard manufacturing the new frame for the building. The new factory enabled the company to move into Industrial and Commercial buildings; the first job was a new printing works for The Nottingham Evening Post at Sutton in Ashfield. The company had earlier completed a new farm building for the Chairman, Colonel Foreman Hardy at Car Colston.

The Evening Post building launched Caunton onto the national scene; it was now invited by Norman Rowan, another Nottingham steelwork company, to join the British Constructional Steelwork Association. At the same time as moving into the industrial buildings market Caunton's also

Top left and top right: *G. Wilkinson, Gary Holden and Ernest Hayes. The Blacksmith's shop was too small for fabricating buildings so all work was carried out in the yard which was formed by utilising the old cottage gardens.* **Above:** *New factory for Caunton being built in the Kirkby in Ashfield Colliery Manager's garden.* **Right:** *The factory on Lowmoor Road, Kirby, built in 1973.*

from the U.S.A. Logistics and 'Just in Time' manufacturing from Japan and 'Can Do' from Australia. The dedicated workforce were willing to change, to take on new technology and move forward. The only thing wrong was that the much-expanded Kirkby factory was now too small.

After a long search the redundant British Coal National Workshops at Moorgreen was acquired. When Caunton's moved in January 1990 there was only one man left out of the 1,500 who had once worked there.

became very active working for Boots at its Beeston main base, and also Island Street in Nottingham. British Coal was another regular client, at one time making up 25% of Caunton's sales.

As well as buildings the company manufactured hoppers, spiral chutes and conveyors. At this time John Deakin was managing the technical office and works, Ray Turton was works foreman, David Bingham on accounts and sales and Tom Broadberry ran the site operations.

A new sales manager, Steve Price was appointed. Coming from an industrial background he soon built up a healthy order book with Brian Fidler doing the quotations. The system required two people to sign off a quotation prior to submission: on one occasion a highly priced job elicited a phone call from an unhappy client saying 'I will report you to Esther Rantzen'

'She won't be interested in you not wanting to pay a fair amount for the work' was Steve's reply.

'She will when she sees a copy of your quotation signed Messrs Fidler and Price!' came the swift response.

By 1978 the company was outgrowing its premises again and serious strain was put on the design office. It was decided to investigate computer aided design—CAD.

Immediately the information blockage was cleared computerisation made it possible to quickly submit calculations for planning. Computers now also produced monthly job costings, and profit and loss accounts.

In the 1980s further automation was sought. Visits to Germany, Japan, Australia and the U.S.A. produced new ideas. New machinery would be German. Simplifying manufacture came

Caunton's set about the task of turning the ghost works into the most advanced factory in the world. By the time the job was completed in 1992 some £3.5 million had been spent on the plant.

By 1993 the plant was fully CAD, CAM and Just in Time manufacturing. The whole industry was racked with recession but Caunton's investment enabled it to move from producing 3,500 tonnes of steel per annum to 12,000 tonnes with the same number of staff.

The company was now a national fabricator with work from Aberdeen oil rigs to Lands End, where it built the last tin mine in the UK. In 1992 all production moved to a Just in Time basis supported by British Steel (now Corus). At the same time one of the original founders, Tom Broadberry retired and the Bingham family purchased all the shares in the business. Also in 1992 Simon Bingham joined

Top left: *Nottingham Evening Post printing works, Sutton in Ashfield.* **Left:** *Factory for making CDs, Thorn EMI Hayes, 1984.* **Above:** *Kirkby in Ashfield factory, 1989.*

staff who work on or visit site now comply with the MCG requirement for CSCS cards.

Within the manufacturing unit, the installation of a CNC tube profiling machine extends the ability to satisfy clients' ever-increasing needs. Team development within the plant and the introduction of multi-skilling has enhanced the capability of Caunton's speedline style production with year-on-year productivity gains.

the company becoming Group M.D. in 1996, and MD of Caunton Engineering in 2000.

Growth from 1992 was a consistent upward path. The company was by now undertaking large nationally noted projects like the new Land Rover plant at Solihull and the Thames Court award-winning building in the City of London, both well in excess of

The company's reputation within the automotive industry has been maintained with the recent addition to its client base of Japanese car giant, Honda, based in Swindon. Caunton has benefited from steelwork's increased success in the residential market. Internal technical capabilities have enabled the company to capture a significant share of this market, while retaining its grip on the retail market and the distribution sector with numerous projects for well-known high street names such as Sainsbury, Asda, IKEA and NEXT.

The development of the use of I.T. across all areas of the business continues to reap rewards, as ever more efficient ways of processing workload are found.

Between 2005 and 2008 the Group purchased a further 32 acres of land. In addition Caunton's invested £5m in a new building and replacement machinery. The new facility, known as Plane Building was opened by the Rt Hon Geoff Hoon and is a 37,000

2,000 tonnes of steel. Shopping centres were completed in Liverpool, Barrow and Mansfield. Tiger Buildings was launched to undertake smaller contracts and service the many partnerships formed with clients and contractors. Tiger's annual sales would exceed £5m.

The year 2001 saw the launch of Caunton's intranet/extranet knowledge portal. Once again the firm was at the cutting edge, harnessing the very latest in technology. A system was created enabling staff, partners, customers and suppliers to access every piece of information held within the company from locations anywhere in the world. With the new millennium came a merger with a sister company, Tiger Buildings Limited, consolidating operations in a fully revamped office.

The company erects over 70% of it output. In the interests of safety and efficiency, the company has played a major role in the development of two major site-oriented innovations – Quicon, the slotted beam-connector, and the Dawson Quick Release beam-lifting safety shackle. Indeed such is the importance of Health and Safety in the company's development plans that all

Top left, top right and above left: Structural steelwork designed delivered and erected throughout Europe. Below: Caunton Engineering Ltd in 2009, Moorgreen, Nottingham. The site covers 42 acres, employs 230 staff and has sales of £38,000,000.

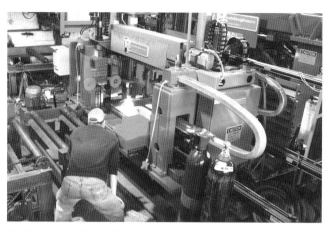

sq.ft development dedicated almost exclusively to state of the art paint application. The development includes energy saving features like solar thermal panels to heat water and roof lights to maximise natural daylight. The latest 'grey water' treatment equipment has also been installed.

Caunton's was awarded the BCSA Silver Award for Sustainability as well as gaining ISO 14001:2004, for environmental management. In 2007 Caunton finalised its Carbon Footprint in readiness for carbon credit trading.

The company has opened its own Academy focused on school leavers and training of key engineering skills alongside a day release college programme. Such has been the success of the scheme that for two consecutive years Caunton's has reached the

high standard, and that investment in engineering and manufacturing resources was progressive and substantial.

On the same night, Caunton's was also awarded a Structural Steel Design Award Certificate of Merit for the Constructionarium Mini-Gherkin, Norfolk.

Today Caunton's is perfectly placed to meet customer expectations in an ever-changing future.

Top left: The staff from February 1970 together for the retirement of Tom Broadberry in 1993. From left: Michael Coulter Tom Broadberry, Alex Coulter and David Bingham. *Top right:* One of the six main CNC machines at the Caunton Plant. All of Caunton's steel is erected on site by the erection department. *Left:* Simon Bingham, Group Managing Director since 2000. Simon joined the company from University and after training in the works, at the Kutsch Steel plant in West and East Germany and The Structural Steel Institute came back to Caunton in 1992. *Left:* One of the six Caunton production lines. *Below:* The site erection team outside the Moorgreen works.

final of the regional apprenticeship of year scheme and more recently was featured on BBC1's Politics Show.

In 2008 Caunton's became Nottinghamshire Company of the Year. The award was sponsored by Nottinghamshire County Council and KPMG; it cited turnover at record levels, training and employee benefits of an exemplary

Boots - Chemists to the Nation

Ask anyone to name a chemist and the odds are that they will immediately say 'Boots'. The name Boots is not only synonymous with High Street pharmacy it is also, thanks to Jesse Boot, a name synonymous with the city of Nottingham.

Early days

The Boots story begins however not with Jesse Boot but his father, John.

John Boot was born in Radcliffe-On-Trent in 1815. His early life was spent as an agricultural labourer on local farms. By 1851 he had moved to Woolpack Lane in Hockley. It was a poor area and John Boot became involved in chapel affairs and local schemes to improve living conditions.

In those days herbal remedies were popular with those who could not afford the services of a doctor. John Boot's mother had used herbs for healing and he may also have been familiar with remedies published in John Wesley's book 'Primitive Physic'. In 1849, with the assistance of his father-in-law and the support of the local Methodist community, John opened The British and American Botanic Establishment at 6, Goose Gate.

In addition to giving consultations and serving in the shop, John and his wife, Mary, prepared many remedies themselves. When John Boot died in 1860, at the age of 45, Mary took over the business with the help of her ten year-old son, Jesse.

The Jesse Boot Era, 1871-1920

When Jesse Boot reached the age of 21 he became a partner in the business, which now traded under the name of M & J Boot, Herbalists. He was determined to cut his prices and asked customers to pay cash rather than offering them credit. Jesse Boot advertised extensively and began to sell an ever wider range of stock; 'over 2,000 articles' as one advert claimed. In 1877 Jesse took sole control and with takings of £100 a week, he became one of the busiest shopkeepers and the largest dealer in patent medicines in Nottingham.

In 1881 a property at 16-20 Goose Gate fell vacant. With financial support from several local business contacts, Jesse Boot took on the lease, and converted the building into a new shop. It contained the retail and wholesale shops, workshops, stockrooms, offices and living accommodation. In 1883 Jesse formed Boot and Company Limited, with himself as Chairman and Managing Director.

After expanding the Goose Gate shop, Jesse Boot wanted to repeat its success. He bought up vacant properties across Nottingham, often sites in poorer districts where properties were reasonably cheap and refurbished them in a characteristic style. Each new shop was opened to a fanfare of publicity. The first Boots store outside Nottingham was opened in 1884, in Lincoln.

*Above: Jesse and Florence Boot, 1886. **Left:** Very early advertising. **Below:** London Road store, Nottingham, 1890s.*

Left: 16-20 Goose Gate, Nottingham, 1885. **Bottom left:** *Pharmacist, 1890.* **Below:** *Advert, 1900.* **Below, centre page:** *Island Street, showing the Fine Chemical and Pharmaceutical Works, 1923.*

Success provoked a hostile reaction from many fellow chemists, who criticised Jesse's cut-price tactics and tried to cast doubt on some of Boot's products. In 1879 the House of Lords had supported the right of general stores and companies, as well as traditional chemists, to dispense prescription medicines. In 1884 Jesse brought in a qualified pharmacist to offer dispensing services; Edwin Waring was appointed, bringing with him the professional prestige that the business needed. True to his business philosophy, Jesse offered this service at half the price normally charged. To build up public confidence in the quality of his products, Jesse renamed the business Boots Pure Drug Company Ltd in 1888.

In 1885 Jesse Boot took a holiday in Jersey, where he met Florence Rowe, the daughter of a bookseller and stationer in St Helier. They were married the following year and John, their first child, was born in 1889.

Florence took an interest in the retail side of the company. New lines were introduced, such as books, stationery, fancy goods, artists' materials and picture frames. Jesse and Florence began to develop a concept of Boots shops as department stores. In

1891 Jesse secured the leasehold of a property at Pelham Street in Nottingham's fashionable town centre. The premises were largely rebuilt, with a gallery supported by a colonnade of cast iron pillars and mahogany counters. Pelham Street became the model for future Boots stores throughout the country.

Meanwhile there was also investment in the manufacturing side of the business. Jesse wanted the company to be fully self-contained so that he could control not only prices but quality. He wanted to be the 'Largest, Best and Cheapest'. In 1885 Jesse took out a lease on three rooms in Island Street in Nottingham. By 1892 he had taken over the whole building and further properties around Island Street and Parkinson Street. Over 80 staff, including a large proportion of women, were employed in packing, bottling, shop fitting, printing, advertising, laboratory work and accounts. The Island Street works, near to the canal, main roads and railway stations, were also ideally sited for developing the company's distribution system.

By 1893 Jesse had opened 33 stores, including seven branches in Nottingham. The business extended further south, into East Anglia, and the West Midlands. At the turn of the century there were nearly 200 stores in the Boots retail chain. In addition to opening new branches, Jesse acquired existing chemist's firms, including William Day's Southern Drug Company, a chain of 60 stores in London and the south of England.

Florence Boot founded a subscription library , the Boots Booklovers' Library, inspired by her interest in literature and the arts. Another idea fostered by Florence, was to open elegant cafes in the larger stores. These had an impact on sales, by attracting the more affluent middle classes to shop at Boots.

The wellbeing of their employees was very important to Jesse and Florence and they provided welfare, education, sports and social facilities for their growing workforce. Meanwhile the Pharmacy Act of 1908 confirmed the legal right of large companies and stores such as Boots to offer dispensing services. In 1911 the National Health Insurance Act led to a dramatic increase in the number of prescriptions.

Jesse Boot was an active member of Nottingham's community, he gave many gifts to the city, including land for public parks and donations to the General Hospital. In 1921 he presented Nottingham's University College with a large plot of land and an endowment fund to help realise their vision of a new campus.

The First World War, 1914 -1918
Boots made a significant contribution to the war effort and produced items for men at the Front, such as water sterilisers, vermin powder and anti-fly cream. Many chemicals such as aspirin and saccharin were previously imported from Germany and Jesse anticipated a shortage in supply. He enlarged the company's laboratories and production facilities and manufactured for the government, domestic and overseas buyers.

American ownership, 1920 -1933
After the war Jesse Boot, increasingly disabled by arthritis, knew he would soon need to relinquish control. In 1920 Louis Liggett, the head of the United Drug Company, one of the largest pharmaceutical firms in America, bought the company for £2.25 million. John Boot, Jesse's son, travelled to America and studied the production methods and organisation of the new parent company. Boots and its 600 stores was re-organised, with a new

*Top left: Boots Head Office on the corner of Station Street and Trent Street in 1920. **Top right:** Tablet granulating at Island Street in the 1920s. **Left:** Pelham Street in 1929. **Centre:** Female employees on board the 'Wembley Special' train to the British Empire Exhibition in 1924. **Above right:** John Boot, son of the founder.*

In 1935 Boot's famous No7 range of cosmetics was launched, in an art deco livery of blue and yellow. To support the new brand, Beauty Parlours were introduced in a number of stores, including Regent Street in London. Soltan suntan lotion was also launched in the 1930's to meet customers demand for a new style of sun protection. The Booklovers' Library also flourished at this time, with branches in 450 stores supporting over half a million subscribers.

committee structure and an emphasis on centralisation and efficiency. The introduction of Territorial General Managers also provided a career structure for pharmacists.

John Boot was associated with most of the new developments within the business and became Chairman in 1927. In 1929 the Depression in America forced L. K. Liggett Co. into bankruptcy. In 1933 the company was sold to a group of British financiers for just over £6m, with John Boot as Chairman and Managing Director.

1930s

The 1,000th Boots store was opened in Galashiels in 1933. This rapid expansion of the retail side of the business meant that factory and warehouse capacity needed to grow as well. A new site at Beeston was acquired between the canal and the railway, reached by a new bridge across the railway line. The first plant to be

built in 1929 was 'D1' the new Soap Works. The 'D' prefix referring to the local area of Dunkirk. The famous 'D10' 'Wets' factory was completed four years later in 1933. It was designed by the engineer Owen Williams and incorporated many advanced and innovative features that influenced the planning of similar structures for decades. The factory was so efficient, that the working week was reduced from 47 1/2 hours to 42 1/2 hours and in 1934 a five day week was introduced, with no cut in pay. Both D10 and the D6 'Drys' factories are now Grade I listed buildings. In 1929 the company also began to establish an agricultural division. In 1934 Lord Trent, as John Boot now was, purchased the Ardnamurchan Estate in Argyll, Scotland, part of which was farmed by the company, to help research and development of horticultural and veterinary products.

Jesse Boot, 1st Baron Trent, died on 13th June 1931.

The Second World War 1939 -1945

During the Second World War as many as 7,000 Boots employees were away on war duty. By the end of the war 381 members of staff had been killed in battle or air raids and 33 shops were destroyed due to enemy action. Some stores were used as First Aid posts and Boots staff also took the Civil Defence ARP test and worked as Air Raid Wardens.

Boots manufacturing capacity was vital to the war effort. 3,000,000 lbs of saccharin was produced (the equivalent of 731,000 tons of sugar, a commodity which was strictly rationed). Some 1,500 tons of Chloramine was produced, for water sterilisation in Europe, Africa and the Far East.

Top Left: Lorries parked in the Transport Department at Island Street in 1924. Centre: 1937 advertising for the famous Boots No7 range, a Boots Soltan information leaflet from 1939 and Boots medicine advertising from 1940. Below: Beeston's D10 building in the late 1930s.

Boots pioneered the manufacture of penicillin in the largest surface culture plant in the world, designed and managed on behalf of the Ministry of Supply. Pharmaceutical research continued; of the 29 new products, 12 had previously been manufactured only in Germany.

Post-war regeneration and new development 1945 - 1968

A programme of factory development in Nottingham was begun following the war, the major part being completed by 1953. This included a new power house, printing works, and, in 1959 a new pharmaceutical research building. In 1949 a factory for the manufacture of cosmetics was opened at Airdrie in Scotland.

The company's agricultural division also expanded; by 1952 Boots was farming 4,500 acres in England and Scotland. New laboratories for horticultural research at Lenton, Nottingham and Thurgarton were completed in 1947. There was also expansion overseas. A retail company had been formed in New Zealand in 1936; and over the next 30 years manufacturing businesses were established in India, Pakistan, Australia and Canada.

There were developments in the world of pharmacy and retailing too: 1948 saw the inauguration of the National Health Service. This led to a vast increase in dispensing and the demand for medicines. In the 1950s some self-service stores were opened and other branches were re-modelled to give partial self-service. In 1965 however, it was announced that the Booklovers' Library was to close.

John Boot had died in March, 1956. Like his father, he was a philanthropist who was keenly involved with the City of Nottingham and also became a national spokesman on Industrial Welfare.

In 1968 a new Head Office, designed by Skidmore, Owings and Merrill of Chicago, was built on the Beeston site, housing over 1,000 people. This is now a Grade II listed building.

The Modern Era

Boots has continued to develop its product ranges. '17' cosmetics was launched in 1968. The analgesic, ibuprofen was introduced in 1969,

Top left: English class at Boots College, 1940s/1950s. *Above:* Inside the Lister Gate store, 1950s. *Centre:* Early advertising for Boots 17 cosmetics. *Below:* Pelham Street, 1960s.

Now that Boots is part of Alliance Boots, the aim is to make Boots a leading global brand and the teams are on track to make this happen.

An exciting future lies ahead for the Boots brand and thanks to Jesse Boot, his name and that of the city of Nottingham will forever be linked.

Top: *19 Lower Parliament Street in 1961.* **Left:** *The new store in the Victoria Centre in 1972.* **Below:** *The entrance to the Victoria Centre store, 1990s.*

and launched as the 'Over the Counter' brand, Nurofen in 1983. There have been several relaunches of No7 cosmetics, and new additions such as Botanics and Natural Collection.

The company also introduced new services. Boots Opticians, formed in 1987, has become one of the UK's leading chain of opticians. Insurance services and other innovative ventures were also pioneered.

In 2006 Boots Group merged with Alliance UniChem to form Alliance Boots, an international pharmacy-led health and beauty group. In June 2007 Alliance Boots was acquired by AB Acquisitions Limited. Following the merger, the development of the Boots brand has been accelerated and the Boots name has never been so widespread.

Sandicliffe Garage - A Great Motoring Family

Nottingham-based Sandicliffe Garage Limited was founded in 1948 by Mr. J R Woodhouse and Mr. T H Barton as a service station on Nottingham Road, Stapleford. The Company became Ford Retail Dealers in 1953. In 1955 a Ford Car and Commercial Vehicle franchise was attained. Things progressed steadily and in 1978, the Royal Warrant of Her Majesty Queen Elizabeth II was granted to the Stapleford Dealership - a rare event in the motor industry.

Mr. J R Woodhouse

Mr. T H Barton

From small beginnings Sandicliffe has expanded to become one of the country's largest privately owned family motor groups with over 600 employees operating from twelve sites located throughout the East Midlands.

The Woodhouse family could trace its roots back to the 17th century when one 'Henorry' Woodhouse a local farmer died in 1660. Records do not go back any further, but it is safe to assume that 'Henorry' was himself the son of a local farmer with many generations before him farming in the area.

J R Woodhouse, known as Richard, was born at Manor Farm, Bilborough – now a community centre for the Aspley housing estate – and grew up in a land of plenty despite the hard times which most of the country was experiencing. Though what there was plenty of according to Richard was "plenty of fresh air, plenty of hard work and plenty of hours in each day!"

Horses were by then giving way to tractors and other motorised vehicles on Britain's farms. At Manor Farm Richard was the only one of three brothers to show any interest in the workings of these new-fangled machines.

When the second world war came everyone was called upon to do their bit. "There were three strapping farm lads at Bilborough and I thought that at least one of us should go and fight for his country, so in 1942 I volunteered" Richard would later recall.

At that time Richard was working "all day and half the night" for the £5 paid to him each week by his father. That stopped after he joined up and exchanged the green fields of Nottinghamshire for the stifling heat and humidity of British India.

Having decided to pursue his interest in vehicles Richard had had joined the Royal Army Ordnance Corps.

Richard's war years were spent repairing tanks and other vehicles pulled out of the Burma campaign where British forces were fighting the Japanese. He rose to become Warrant Officer Class 1, but three times failed to become an officer

Top: Founders, Mr Richard Woodhouse (left) and Mr Henry Barton. Left: Sandicliffe garage and forecourt in Nottingham Road, Stapleford in 1949. Above: A Sandicliffe stand for a 1960s open air motor show at Wollaton Park.

but moved to Nottinghamshire to take up farming; they had also set up an early bus service in 1908 which would eventually expand enormously to become Barton Transport.

Richard Woodhouse and Henry Barton had played together as children, attended the same school and remained good friends. That friendship was further cemented in 1943 when Richard married Henry's sister, Evelyn.

Henry had shown no inclination to join his family's business despite being steeped in the knowledge of what went on under the bonnets of cars and lorries.

It seemed only natural when one day in 1947 Richard asked Henry to join him in the motor trade.

The two friends' application for a licence to run a new coach service to Northern Ireland was turned down after concerted pressure from other bus companies; they soon realised they were on the wrong track.

It was now 1948 and the pair had bought a small garage in Stapleford.

Stapleford was a perfect location since Henry Barton lived in Chilwell and Richard Woodhouse now lived in Bramcote on his

Top left: Stapleford Garage in the early days. Left: Diagnosis test setting in the 1950s. Below: The parts department pictured in the 1950s.

because he was not regarded by the army hierarchy as good enough to command and lead men. It was an assessment which would certainly be challenged by future events when Richard would eventually come to manage a small army of employees.

With peace however, came a return to Bilborough and the farm. The work had not changed nor had the wages. There was still plenty of fresh air and his father still paid him £5 a week for nearly 20 hours work every day.

Soon however, it was obvious that farming was not Richard's ambition and a chance conversation with a childhood chum, teenage mate and adult friend, Henry Barton, set the ball rolling.

Henry Barton was the son of another farmer. The Bartons had been quarry owners in Derbyshire

father's extended farm. With their dreams of obtaining an operators' licence to run coaches between Nottingham and Ireland now in tatters the friends decided to set up a small vehicle repairs business and petrol station.

The work was not very lucrative, because throughout Britain at the time there were approximately one million vehicles on the road and whilst petrol was relatively inexpensive, the profit magin was low. Hard work however, had its reward. The working day started at 7am and finished at 11 pm when Richard would stop manning the petrol pumps and retire to the workshop to mend punctures until the early hours of the morning. Two months after the business started a young man, Alan Richards, was taken on to learn the trade as an apprentice. There was a touch of Henry Ford about Richard Woodhouse. Ford's powerful face looked down on Richard in his office with a similar expression of grit and determination etched on each visage.

In the early 1950s Cartergate Motor Co. in Nottingham was the main Ford dealer in the area – though sharing the Nottinghamshire franchise with Evinsons. Although Richard Woodhouse and Henry Barton were repairing and servicing every type of vehicle on the road they decided to 'go Ford' because they were low priced and the pair believed that low-cost mass-produced cars were likely to sell in greater volume.

In 1953 the partners gained the sub-dealership from the Cartergate Motor Co. for the Stapleford and Beeston area; but

Top and below: *Views of Sandicliffe, Nottingham Road, in the 1960s and 1970s.* **Above:** *Testing in the 1970s.*

Left and below: *Sandicliffe's Loughborough (left) and Stapleford premises in the 1970s.* **Bottom:** *Sandicliffe cars on view at the Moorgreen Show, 1970s.*

the arrangement meant they could only sell four new cars a year.

The two friends decided to do what most garages with franchises shied away from and moved into the used car market. With four new cars sold a year this effectively doubled car sales because people who bought new often traded in vehicles which could then be sold second hand.

In those post-war years the demand for new cars far outstripped supply and priorities were imposed – with a number of doctors and nurses receiving the Sandicliffe allocation in the firm's early days.

Demand at Sandicliffe prompted Richard Woodhouse to approach Ford's UK headquarters with a view to becoming a

main dealer. The giant company's bureaucratic wheels began turning and a survey was carried out.

The result was refusal for Sandicliffe because it was not thought there was enough room for another main dealer in the area. The Henry Ford in Richard Woodhouse bubbled to the top and he wrote to Ford's Chief executive in Britain telling him he did not know his job. The letter certainly had an impact: the two partners were summoned to the Chief

Executive's office to explain their impertinence. "I just wanted to see the two young boys who tell me I do not know how to run my job" he told them. Undeterred Richard and Henry explained their reasons for writing. The conclusion was that they were told that from August 1955 they would be main dealers!

It was not a decision Ford would regret. If they had been turned down Richard and Henry would have immediately tried for a British Leyland Franchise.

Repairing and selling cars were only two sides of the business. The firm had also been dealing with lorries and vans since it had started.

An increasing number of vehicles on the road meant expansion at the garage. A truck depot was now formed at Stapleford which meant demolishing Richard Woodhouse's former home. The expansion began to speed up, and in 1962 Sandicliffe moved to Ilkeston. Ford had been looking for a main dealership for South-East Derbyshire. A good job done at

Stapleford since the early days resulted in the car giant granting the new franchise to Sandicliffe. Sub dealerships were in turn granted by Sandicliffe to garages in Codnor, Langley Mill and Eastwood.

Three years later Sandicliffe bought out Gillotts Garage in Loughborough which already had a Ford franchise. Happily Ford approved the takeover by granting a transfer of its franchise. Next on the list of acquisitions was the Boston Motor Company in 1975 followed by an enterprise in Long Eaton in 1978. The foundation of the Sandicliffe Group was based on commonsense, and the Group's policy has changed little since those days. Both partners had a keen interest in vehicles. Experience helped, but even by the time the business began to grow their knowledge was still less than expert. An early priority was to gather together a staff of top class mechanics: the continuation of that policy remains one of the Group's greatest assets.

Honesty too has been a fundamental business principle. According to Richard Woodhouse "Honesty is the best policy. If we had anyone bordering on the corrupt in any way we would have failed. In fact we have always done everything above the law." It has been this belief which has set

Top left: Sandicliffe's van and truck sales, 1970s. Centre: A selection of vehicles manufacturers available from Sandicliffe Garages. Below: The services department at Sandicliffe.

In 2005 Sandicliffe expanded by taking over both Ford and Suzuki franchises in Hucknall to create a new area of business activity in North Nottinghamshire. In June that same year a Basford dealership joined the Group adding Mazda, Fiat and Kia to the franchise. The following year the Nottingham City and Daybrook Ford franchises became the latest acquisitions. Operating from Loughborough Road, West Bridgford they underline Sandicliffe's position as one the region's leading Dealer groups.

Sandicliffe staff apart from the popular idea of the car salesman. Richard agreed that every trade has its black sheep, but Sandicliffe set higher standards. "By doing so we have probably missed making a million a lot of times, but it is good to go home and put my head on the pillow and think what a wonderful example we have set by doing things the right way". "The customer will always find the black sheep out and they will not go back to them, while I am still selling cars to people who found they had a flat tyre and brought it to me in 1948."

The turnover in car sales is complicated. About 60 per cent of new vehicles are sold to business fleets, the rest are sold through finance and loan agreements.

Neither Richard Woodhouse nor Henry Barton had any training in accounts and it is to their credit that they first applied commonsense and then brought in men who knew the intricacies of making money work. In 1948 the turnover of the first year of trading was just £1,700. Net profit was a mere £125 with which to pay the two partners and their apprentice. No one back then could have predicted the scale of future developments.

During 1995 a Melton Mowbray dealership joined the Group. Though the Boston and Ilkeston dealerships were later sold these were matched by new dealerships in Market Harborough and Leicester.

By the 21st century the business would enjoy a multi-million pound turnover, 600 employees and sales of more than 12,000 cars a year. Ford would not however, hold complete sway over the business forever. The Sandicliffe Group now offers a complete range of motoring services including New and Used Cars and Commercials, Parts, Service, Accident Repair and Fleet, and in addition to its Ford franchises also holds new vehicle franchises for Mazda, Fiat, Kia and Suzuki.

Today Richard Woodhouse' eldest son Andrew is Chairman of the Sandicliffe Group (www.sandicliffe.co.uk.); Andrew's brother Nicholas is also a Director, alongside Henry Barton's son Thomas Barton.

In the 21st century the business is still a family firm, the latest member to join the team is Andrew Woodhouse' son Paul.

BY APPOINTMENT
TO HER MAJESTY THE QUEEN
SUPPLIERS OF MOTOR HORSE BOXES
AND AUTOMOBILE ENGINEERS
SANDICLIFFE GARAGE LTD. OF STAPLEFORD

Top, left and top right: *Sandicliffe Garage, Nottingham Road, Stapleford, Nottingham.* **Centre:** *The Royal Warrant of her majesty Queen Elizabeth II.* **Below:** *Todays Board, from left to right, Mr Tom Barton, Director, Mr Nicholas Woodhouse, Company Secretary, and Mr Andrew Woodhouse, Chairman.*

Perfectos - Perfect Inks

Perfectos Speciality Inks Ltd. based in Normanton Lane, Bottesford, has become a name indelibly linked with Nottinghamshire.

With a loyal staff of 45 Perefectos is the largest employer in Bottesford and the surrounding area. Many members of staff have over 10, 20, and even 40 years of service behind them.

Making ink is a surprisingly hi-tech activity. The firm was founded by John Henry Price, a qualified research and development chemist. Educated initially at Mansfield Secondary Technical School, then at the People's College Nottingham, John Price later attended Nottingham Trent University part-time to earn a degree in Nuclear Physics and Radiochemistry. His degree qualified him for admission to the Royal Institute of Chemistry.

John Price was born in 1943 in Kirkby-in-Ashfield, Nottinghamshire. He founded his own business in 1969 at the age of 26. At that time he was still working for Farbwerke Hoechst AG, (a large German dyestuffs, pigments and chemicals manufacturer based in Frankfurt). John worked in the UK for Farbwerke Hoechst as a technical sales rep.

Previously John had worked at Boots in its Support and Plant laboratories at Nottingham and Beeston Works. There he assisted chemists and works engineers in Quality Control and Product Development for the manufacturing of many of their special ranges of cosmetics, pharmaceuticals, soaps and organic chemicals such as saccharin, potassium permanganate, aspirin, heparin, cortisone and ibuprofen.

After working for Boots Chemicals for five years John had then joined P P Payne of Haydn Road, Nottingham, a large and well known company producing speciality packaging tapes, tear-tapes, industrial packaging, strapping of non-metallic types, and fabric labels of all types for clothes, bedding, mattresses and carpets.

John was initially employed at P P Payne to set up its virtually non-existent Quality Control system. As soon as that was up and running well, John was asked to develop special types of printing inks never made before, inks which had to have many very specific properties.

John was employed for some five years as a development chemist at P P Payne, and whilst there developed printing inks

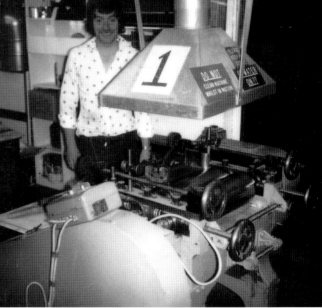

*Top: Founder, John Price and wife Ann. **Left:** Starting up - the Price's garage in 1970. **Above:** Employee Stu Gunn working at the original factory in Bottesford in the mid-1970s.*

Hoechst but wanted to 'test the water'. He decided to have a go at ink development and manufacture in his garage at nights and weekends to see if this might be a viable business.

The whole enterprise was set up with £50 capital from John himself, and an interest-free loan from his parents of a further £50.

This quickly became a very busy time for John. After working all day selling colourants, dyestuffs and pigments, he started work in the garage at 6pm after a quick dinner, sometimes not finishing until 2am.

John's wife Ann was soon drawn into the new enterprise, answering the phone, delivering ink to customers, and helping obtain empty boxes from the Co-op and other local shops to send the ink out in.

for the firm, despite the fact that he had had no previous training in ink technology. Training was 'on the job'. It was John's mindset of inquisitiveness and meticulous attention to detail that produced the correct properties required by both the printers and the end users. He successfully developed inks for the fabric garment label trade, as P P Payne was at that time the main UK supplier of printed fabric care labels used in the garment industry.

Nottingham and Leicester were both large manufacturing bases for the Textile and Hosiery trade which used the fabric care labels Paynes produced. Today however, much of that trade has now been dispersed to the Far East, India and China and to other countries where low-cost labour and low taxes are available.

Above: A view inside the Bottesford garage in the 1970s.
Bottom left: A brochure cover showing companies who use Perfectos products. Below: Ink stocks in the 1980s.

Whilst he was working for Farbwerke Hoechst AG John Price was asked to produce printing inks for people who knew he was a chemist and had produced inks whilst at P P Payne. They were keen to have a superior product developed and made by John, now an acknowledged expert, to compete in the marketplace.

John was in a well paid and interesting job with

The business name was thought up during dinner one night, when Ann suggested they should have a 'perfect product'. The name PERFECTOS soon developed from that.

At busy times Ann was also co-opted to mix and mill (refine) the inks whilst John was busy on other things.

In the first year the small business already had a turnover of £3,000.

As the demand became greater it was no longer possible to make sufficient ink on the 'Night shift'. A full time worker was employed as John still wanted to keep safe and to continue working for Hoechst in case the business did not prove successful. Meanwhile 18 hour days and seven day weeks became no strangers to John and Ann.

After five years of very hard work by everybody turnover had increased to over £50,000 and two full time and four or five part time staff were employed - and they were still running out of time, and ink.

During those years Ann provided lunches for all the workers, and moral support for the weekend staff.

John was a good salesman. He was trained by Heinz-Goldmann, a world famous sales training organisation whilst working for Farbwerke Hoechst. Whilst there he had increased his Midlands patch turnover from around £3,000 to well over £3 million within four years. He was sent on many sales training courses for extended periods, to learn all the 'tricks-of-the-trade' of salesmanship. As time went on a career selling his own products finally beckoned.

By now John's home-made 'Perfectos' inks were becoming famous and much in demand as the print didn't wash-off the

*Above: The 'Boss' checks the mills in the 1980s. **Left:** Celebrating Perfectos' 18th year, December 1987. **Below:** Stu Gunn and Walter Blohm (the company's Brazilian agent) at a Perfectos exhibition in Sao Paulo, Brazil, in the mid-1980s showing the ROTAFAB Mk.II printing machine and inks.*

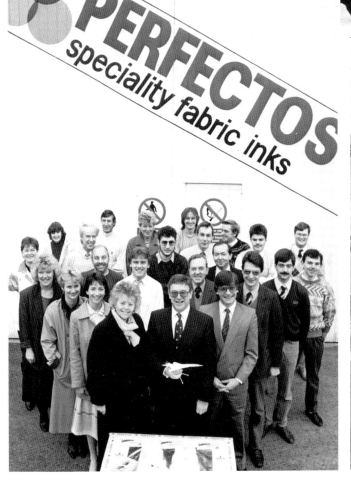

pigments and other raw materials began to be stored in the house and loft.

Ann then spent a lot of her time looking for a house somewhere nearby with a larger garage and possible space for expansion, and more sheds or a further garage. She eventually found an old mill in Bottesford, fell in love with the property and it was bought within a month.

John's father bought the house in Arnold from John and Ann so the company could continue to manufacture there for the time being until it was ready to produce ink at Bottesford.

labels during washing and dry-cleaning. The inks were being specified on fabric care labels for clothes produced for many leading stores, such as Marks & Spencer, Adams, Boots, Ladybird, BHS, Littlewoods and C&A.

The word was out. Perfectos even started to sell overseas, with a good business in Denmark, the USA and Japan.

Many people however, had made significant contributions to the increasing reputation and status of the firm.

Stu Gunn started as a part-time worker in 1971, and still works for the company today in the role of Technical Service in the R&D Labs. Ivan Cresswell, who also started in 1971 and has recently retired, worked in most areas of production.

John's father, who died in July 2009 aged 88 years, worked for the company for over ten years in various manufacturing and 'Jack-of-all-trades jobs' before retiring in 1984.

By the early 1970s the company was occupying not only a garage but also two garden sheds in Arnold at the side of John and Ann's house. They made inks there for almost four years until Ann put her foot down when

When they moved to Bottesford, Ann wanted a washing machine plumbed in. Stopping the car to ask a man for directions, he turned out to be a plumber. Mr Eric Pacey not only plumbed in the washing machine but also knew someone who could refit a door - Ken Pacey, a joiner. He also knew Mick Pacey who happened to be a bricklayer who could fix a new wall. And Mick Pacey had a brother, Roger Pacey the 'metal man' who could fix anything, and now made some metal gates for John and Ann. What a team, and what an excellent find.

Top left: *In the laboratory in 1986.* **Above:** *Two views of Perfectos Mills in the 1980s.* **Left:** *John Price watches on as the first lift is installed at Bottesford.*

However, there was no room for an office in the new unit which therefore had to remain in John and Ann's home. This became so impractical that a couple of years later more space was rented and the office was moved. Home was finally now home!

In 1987, after 18 years in business, John and Ann took all the firm's employees and their partners together with several suppliers and advisors on a trip on Concorde including a Christmas meal and a visit to the London Christmas lights. This was very well received; Andrea Bradley, one of the firm's first secretaries, even baked a large cake for the occasion.

So started a 35 year plus relationship with "PACEYS & CO" who have virtually worked for both the company, and for John and Ann privately, ever since.

It would have been difficult to have succeeded without their help which would be available on a 24/7 basis ever since that first fortuitous encounter. The Paceys would make many bespoke items of plant and equipment. They have also done a great deal of building work for Perfectos. By 2009 they were in the process of building a new garage block and extension.

Exports now began to take an increasing role. Back in 1975 all sales were in the UK. As the 'rag trade' slowly but surely moved overseas to less expensive manufacturing bases Perfectos' customers set up there also, making the garment labels locally. Perfectos began to supply them with its quality inks for their washable labels made overseas. Meanwhile, a couple of years after moving to Bottesford, and increasing growth, it became decision time again. The firm decided to rent a small portion of a factory unit on the local industrial estate, and finally move away from home.

Over the years production has increased and the product range has widened, though with the emphasis still on speciality inks, and always in relatively small volumes by other ink makers' standards.

The ink range now includes: Rotary and Flatbed Letterpress Fabric Label Inks, Silk-screen Fabric inks, Flexographic Fabric Inks, Heat Transfer inks for Sports and Fashion use, Stretchable

Top left: The Ink Blending area pictured in the 1990s.
Above: A Rotafab Mk.III label printing machine of 1993.
Left: Terry Deverill milling one of his last batches of ink, 1997/1998.

water based heat-transferable inks, Security Inks for various uses, Inks for Reflective surfaces for, the Police/Ambulance and Fire Services "Hi-Viz"clothing and equipment use.

Key components of the company's business philosophy include:
Never use raw materials other than the best.
Always ensure the quality is right first time every time
Always ensure deliveries are on time, every time
Remember "we have 'solutions' NOT 'problems' "

And Perefectos 'trade secrets' include never to using phrases such as "It's the exchange rate"; "You can't do it"; "It'll never sell"; "It won't work"; "They won't want it" or "It can't be done".

Today the company is run and operated by a new generation. Steven Price, in his capacity as Managing Director has full control of day-to-day operations. John Price now takes a back-seat as Company Chairman, but keeps an eye on financial matters, and still keeps up an interest in the R&D work. He also likes to keep a check on the progress of current investments, not least the building and reorganisation of a new factory which is being masterminded by Steven. New manufacturing techniques and cutting edge technology and equipment are also being used in order to increase production capacity and keep costs down.

Perfectos boasts the only lift in Bottesford, a design copied from the Jaguar car factory where Edward Price, John and Ann's youngest son, worked at the time as a computer engineer. The lift has saved thousands of hours and backache in moving goods up and down in the two floor factory.

Steven is a dynamic character who works long hours and is passionate about keeping costs down, recycling of waste and being 'Eco friendly'. Most of the inks are either water-based, or have very low levels of volatile organic compounds, which do not harm the environment.

Steven was educated at Bottesford Primary School and then went on to Trent College in Long Eaton, before studying full time at Watford College to gain a B.Sc. (Hons) (First Class) in Printing & Packaging Technology. He learned not only about inks technology, but also ideas about computerisation, ideas which have since been heartily embraced by Perfectos.

Steven then went to work at other inkmakers in Hull and Birmingham to experience the business at the 'front end' and gain valuable insight into the inks business.

Before joining Perfectos however, Steven moved to South Africa where he set up his own Property Sales company in Cape Town, and later established a similar business in Tenerife.

Turnover at Perfectos is now approaching £5million per annum, with 90% of sales going to export.

The next page in the Perfectos story may well be expanding production overseas under direct supervision from Bottesford.

Above: View of the Ink Milling (Grinding) Section in 1999. Left: A bird's eye view of Perfectos Mills, Normanton Lane, Bottesford, Nottingham. Below: Three generations of the Price family at the current factory. Pictured is founder John Price (back), his parents Barbara and Harry Price and his son, the current Managing Director, Steven Price.

H Sladen & Son Ltd - On the Road to Fame

The haulage firm of H Sladen & Son Ltd, today based on Daniel's Way at Hucknall, just off the M1, is one of the area's longest established businesses. The company has a proud reputation for customer service and satisfaction – a reputation built up over three generations.

It was back in the 1920s that the firm's founder Harold Sladen first set up in business for himself. The same family has run the company ever since. Today Harold's son David is Chairman and his grandson Robert is Managing Director.

In March 1927, after ten years down the mines, and more time spent out of work than in work, Harold Sladen borrowed £170 from his father and bought a small coal delivery business with a horse and cart and twelve coal customers.

It is a remarkable testimony to Harold Sladen that he should have made the business succeed. Though prospects might not have looked too bad in 1927 the situation two years later was very different. The Wall Street Crash of 1929 heralded a worldwide slump of unprecedented severity. Britain's towns and cities, not least Nottingham, were not immune to the global economic slump. Unemployment escalated to unheard of heights whilst the Government despaired of finding a solution.

By dint of honest hard work and initiative however, Harold was able to buck the trend. The fact that his main activity involved coal certainly helped him. In the 1930s Britain was still a coal powered nation, and whilst many luxuries might be done without, no one could do without coal to fuel boilers and steam engines or to heat their homes.

In 1930 Harold bought his first lorry, a 30cwt. Chevrolet, which was the forerunner of the Bedford lorry.

Meanwhile Harold was a man of strong principles and would not get married whilst he still owed money and the business was not secure. As a consequence he did not marry his wife Daisy until 1934. She had been personal secretary to Mr Milne, who was the Company Secretary of the Boots Co., Nottingham, and was therefore able to do the book-keeping for the business, which was now growing.

H. SLADEN, Junr.,

Coal Merchant & Carting Contractor

Personal Attention to all orders.

133, RADFORD BOULEVARD, NOTTINGHAM.

Top left: Harold Sladen, founder of the company. **Top right:** This hand painted advertisement for the company was printed when the company was founded in 1927. **Left:** One of the delivery lorries from the 1950s outside a customer's premises. **Above:** Harold Sladen's first company business card from 1927.

day with two drivers delivering and collecting bulk mail for the Army Post Office. Harold also had a contract transporting prisoners of war to and from work and back to their camp on Wollaton Park.

Whilst the Second World War raged the Labour Party had taken a keen interest in what a post-war Labour Government might do if it could beat Winston Churchill's Conservatives and get elected. It planned to nationalise many industries, promoting a socialist plan to take into public ownership coal mining, railways, steel and many other industries – amongst them road haulage firms.

After the war ended in 1945 Harold's brother, Wilf Sladen, came to work for him and together they developed the coal business and with the purchase of J. Alvey Coal Merchants, finishing up with 1,300 customers.

When the incoming Labour Government nationalised road haulage firms Harold's relatively small operation, in any event concerned primarily with coal deliveries, was not large enough to be caught in the net of nationalisation.

In 1934 Harold bought his second lorry, which was a 'T' Type Ford with twin back wheels, the first of its kind in Nottingham. However, he did not have much luck with this vehicle as the brakes were not very good - when he parked on a hill in The Park, Nottingham, it ran downhill and crashed into a tree. So much for that vehicle! He returned to using the Chevrolet, and in 1936 he bought a Guy Wolf lorry and this proved to be an excellent vehicle for the job and lasted many years.

The outbreak of war in 1939 brought many difficulties, not least petrol rationing and coal rationing. During the war however, from 1939 to 1945, Harold employed two drivers and even bought another lorry, a Bedford two-tonner, which he fitted with a canvas sheeted body. The lorry worked two shifts per

Road haulage was more of a sideline until denationalisation when Harold bought two 'A' licences and two 'B' licences. This was a unique opportunity – all of the larger pre-war road haulage firms had gone out of existence as a result of post-war Government policy, now however, enterprising folk like Harold could take

Top left: Harold and Daisy Sladen pictured in the 1930s. Left: A joint outing with George Dominic Ltd and Thomas Hind Ltd in the 1950s. Above: David Sladen, son of the founder driving a float in the Nottingham Lord Mayor's Show in the 1970s.

Between 1960 and 1970, with HJ Heinz now a major client and up to five vehicles dedicated just to Boots, the business grew from three vehicles to ten vehicles and outgrew its original premises. The year 1970 saw the business move to Old Basford and to much larger premises.

Company founder Harold Sladen now retired at the age of 68. This was a sad day for him as the business had been his life. His wife Daisy also retired and David's wife Margaret took over the accounting side of the business and now became Company Secretary. New challenges arose almost immediately. Those who lived through the early 1970s will readily recall the three-day week and monetary inflation rising to almost 30 per cent. Most worrying of all to anyone involved in road haulage was the Arab oil embargo and the massive hike in fuel prices. For some time it was even expected that diesel and petrol would have to be rationed as it had been during the war. Happily, David Sladen proved to be as resourceful and energetic as his father in meeting the challenges posed by new problems. If Harold had been able to meet and overcome the difficulties of the 1930s then his son David was quite the man to meet the 1970s with equal vigour. H

advantage of the Government's change of heart. It was a period when many of today's road haulage firms came into existence.

In 1958, David Sladen, Harold's son, came to work in the business and over the next five years the coal side was phased out and eventually sold whilst David developed the haulage side of the firm's operations.

In 1960, the firm became a limited company and H Sladen & Son Ltd was put on to the business map. In 1968 the firm began delivering for the Gerard Soap Works (later to become Cussons.)

Top left: David alongside one of the company's Bedford TM's in the 1980s. Below left: From left to right, today's Managing Director, Robert Sladen, pictured with his parents David and Margaret Sladen. Above: Part of the Sladen & Son fleet in the 1990s. Below: David about to drive into the company's new premises in Daniels Way, Hucknall in April 1998.

By the late 1990s the company had outgrown its Lincoln St, Old Basford premises. H Sladen & Son Ltd moved to a new purpose built depot which included extensive warehouse, parking and garage facilities alongside modern offices at Daniels Way, Hucknall.

Robert Sladen became Managing Director in 2001 when his father David retired from that post to become company Chairman. Today the company has 20 vehicles and 30 trailers. The fleet is constantly replaced and updated, many of which are provided in customers' own liveries.

Sladen & Son began delivery work for Kennelpak in 1974 in Castle Donnington, delivering supplies of pet food all over the country. Now in the 21st century Kennelpak is still a major customer. Other new business opportunities also arose. From the mid-1970s to the mid-1980s RHM would be a major customer in conjunction with Atlas Express.

David Sladen's son Robert joined the company in 1988, starting at the bottom, doing everything, and learning all aspects of the business.

In the 21st century H Sladen & Son Ltd continues to apply the same business philosophy followed by its founder - that excellent customer care and service are the company's first priority.

Meanwhile, who knows, maybe one day Robert and his wife Maria's two young sons will in turn carry on the family business founded so long ago by their great grandfather Harold Sladen.

Early 1990 was a turbulent time for the company with the demise of some very long established customers – one of whom left a very large debt. When that customer got into difficulties it caused serious knock on financial problems for H Sladen. Happily other customers rallied round and helped keep the business afloat. Sladen's were fortunate at this time to have DMW Logistics as a customer, the relationship grew with five vehicles and also trailers in their corporate livery. DMW Logistics, based at Kirkby in Ashfield, have continued to be a major customer.

Indeed, throughout its long history H Sladen & Son Ltd has been fortunate to have some very loyal customers without whom the story could have been very different. In the early 1990s the firm found itself delivering railtrack, crossings and junctions for Balfour Beatty Railway Engineers from Sandiacre to the Channel Tunnel then being built. It also took gun barrels from the Royal Ordnance factory up to Cumbria for test firing out to sea before bringing them back again.

Top left: *David retires in 2001 handing over the reins to son Robert.* **Above left:** *David Sladen (left) is bestowed with Life Membership of the RHA, 2002.* **Above:** *One of the Sladen fleet carrying a customer's own livery trailer.* **Below:** *Sladen's change of livery to white.*

John Pye & Sons - From a Small Acorn to a Mighty Oak

and Government bodies. From small beginnings John Pye & Sons are at the forefront of UK secondary market disposals. With more than 140 auctions a year the company was described by The Sunday Times, in 2008, as one of the biggest UK independent auction house.

The present business has its roots in events more than forty years ago when John and Ann Pye formed 'Furniture and General Auctions', handling mainly livestock, chattels and probate items.

Auctions and auctioneering have been around since time immemorial. During the days of the Roman Empire soldiers would often simply drive a spear into the ground to mark the spot where the spoils of war were to be auctioned off.

These days things are far more sophisticated. In Nottingham the firm of John Pye & Sons has brought the business of auctioneering to heights never dreamed of in centuries past.

Today, based at James Shipstone House in Radford Road, John Pye & Sons Ltd is an international business, dealing not in the simple 'household clearances' and the like of auctioneering days gone by, but with the assets of banks, finance houses, retail PLCs

John Pye's career as an auctioneer began in unpromising fashion. Managers at a horse sale entrusted their junior employee with the disposal of a solitary donkey – then the wretched creature dropped dead. Undeterred by that early set back the pitman's son from Langley Mill went on the build a

Top left: *Founder, John Pye.* **Above:** *John Pye taking an auction at the cattle market in the early days.* **Below inset and below:** *In 1991 the company purchased Heston U Store (inset) adjacent to their Meadow Lane head office (below).*

years later an important milestone was passed when the firm sold its first individual item for more than one million pounds – a Heidelberg printing press sold on behalf of a finance company.

The Redfern Storage and Distribution depot at Trowell was bought in 2000; the site covering some four acres with 40,000 sq ft of space. Two years later the depot was sold on, generating a spectacular 64% profit.

valuation, sales, storage and property consultancy empire with an annual turnover measured in millions.

In 1969 the firm moved into a 1,500 site in the Corn Exchange at the Cattle Market which they leased from Nottingham City Council.

The firm's first 'in situ' sale was held on the instruction of insolvency practitioner Mr J Twigg of Thornton Baker. John Pye managed the sale of 600 items of machinery and stock at the Staffordshire site of two insolvent mechanical engineering firms.

The company name was changed to John Pye & Sons in 1984. Three years later the firm acquired larger premises at the Cattle Market, adding a further 1,800 sq ft to increase the number of auction rooms available to cope with the growth in sales.

A second U-Store was built on the site of James Shipstone House in 2003. Almost 120 purpose built storage units were created increasing the company's storage capacity to 257 units.

Company founder John Pye officially retired on 23rd February 2003, though he remained Chairman and a part-time consultant.

"As a lad I became hooked on the atmosphere of auctions and salesrooms and I'm still addicted" said the 72 two year old after presiding at his last sale.

When he was a boy John Pye had been fascinated by the bidding at Melton Market and was mesmerised by the

Top left: Pye's transport vehicles outside the Meadow Lane premises in the early 1990s. Right: John Pye's first brochure. Left and below: John Pye pictured in the sales compound on view day in 1981 at the sale of county council agricultural machinery, grass cutting machinery and building materials.

John and Ann Pye's son James joined the business in 1989. The following year the firm opened new head offices at Banton House in Meadow Lane.

What was now known as 'JPSL' acquired Heston U-Store, a 40,000 sq ft building to satisfy the firm's growing storage needs. Adam Pye now also joined his parents to work for the company. That same year John Pye was appointed President of the National Association of Auctioneers and Valuers.

In 1995 the former Shiptone's Brewery was acquired, enabling JPSL to establish the largest specialist auctioneering complex in the Midlands. As a result Banton House was now sold. Three

auctioneers' indecipherable staccato delivery. On leaving school in 1944 John went to work for British Ropes at Eastwood, but at the age of 16 he left and went into the clearance and sales trade.

"I borrowed £16 from Stan Brown at the Thorn Tree in Woodinkin to buy a horse and cart" John recalled. "Its name was Spanker." "The idea was the clear stuff from people flitting – moving house – and at home I filled up the back with what my Dad called 'rubbish." "Spanker was just an 11 hands pit pony, but he was a bit lively and it would take you half an hour to round him up from the field. I used to give someone a shilling a week to do that for me".

John then became a booking clerk with the Arnold Graham Horse Sales in Mansfield and it was there that he cut his teeth as an auctioneer.

"I was always asking Mr Graham to let me auction something, and eventually he said yes" John recalled. "Finally Mr Graham said 'All right then, there's a donkey round the pig pen – you can sell that'." The donkey may have dropped dead, but that wasn't enough to deter the would-be auctioneer. "In the end I got seven and sixpence from a slaughterer!"

As things turned out the dead donkey did not mark the immediate elevation of John to the ranks of auctioneers: National service now beckoned. John felt

that he was a natural for the Veterinary Corps. But with all the usual perversity that National Service was famous for John however, instead found himself called up to work as a coal miner. This was a blessing in disguise. The money was surprisingly good. "I started on £8 or £9 but once you were on the face and doing overtime it was fantastic money - £42 a week. As a result I was able to buy a small farm for £1,000."

The hard work did John no harm either – his muscles led to him being a contender for the title of 'UK Amateur Mr Universe'. After doing his stint of National Service John took up dealing in furniture. A great raconteur, John recalls visiting one gloomy gas lit house to buy a four poster bed. "We went into the room and once it was well lit you could see this four poster. It was William IV and I said '£50'. Then, while I was walking around the bed, I noticed that some of the bedclothes were hanging off over the edge so I flipped them up. What I saw made my hair stand on end". I told him "There's a dead man here!" He said "yes we know, I thought we would cop some money before my brothers came round."

*Top: Even back in 1991 Pye's had installed modern sophisticated computing technology in their administration and accounts department, providing them with a comprehensive customer database and mailing list. **Left:** The usual sight of a packed viewing at John Pye & Sons. **Below:** The former Shipstone's Brewery was acquired by the company in 1995 and in a multi-million pound regeneration project, the building was restored back to its former glory.*

Following John's retirement a contract from a UK retail PLC was secured in 2004 supplying weekly stock consignments for auction. John Pye & Sons was appointed to manage large scale retail disposal of residue stock after the closure of 106 High Street stores. Adam Pye was now officially appointed managing director, taking over day to day control of commercial operations.

In 2005 founder and Chairman John Pye celebrated his 75th birthday, two new directors were appointed to the Board: Paul Longson (Operations) and Sheldon Miller (Business Development) and the company developed a new bespoke client web case management system called Assetline, providing an online case diary log of all management and sales

anniversary at a red carpet event held at Wollaton Hall in Nottingham. Staff past and present joined clients from the worlds of insolvency law, banking, fiancé and the retail sector.

John Pye & Sons Ltd opened their Birmingham office in 2009 to meet ever increasing demand and trained two more auctioneers, bringing the company roster to five.

Left: Managing Director, Adam Pye (centre), pictured with Sheldon Miller, Business Development Director (left) and Paul Longson, Operations Director. **Above:** *A bird's eye view of John Pye & Sons 5.2 acre asset, storage and sales facility on Radford Road, Nottingham.* **Below:** *The Pye family pictured toasting the firms 40th anniversary at Wollaton Hall, Nottingham, in 2008. Left to right: James, John, Ann and Adam Pye.*

activity. Auctions increased in frequency from five up to six a month in 2006, as year on year sales roles by 14%. Trevor Palethorpe now became a Deputy Auctioneer to assist Principal Auctioneer Adam Pye. Coinciding with rising sales the firm held the UK's largest ever auction of laptop computers, whilst a leading UK department store chain appointed John Pye & Sons as weekly disposal agents for surplus stock. Auction frequency increased again in 2007 to eight sales a month. New bidding rooms were developed within the old keg plant at the brewery site, providing seating for over 100 buyers with a plasma screen image projection of all lots under the hammer.

In 2008, as the credit crunch took hold of the world economy, John Pye & Sons became the focus of media interest. The Financial Times, Sunday Times, The Guardian and the BBC all noted the company's remarkable progress. A third sale room was now developed to accommodate the overspill of saleable assets. Meanwhile the company celebrated its 40th

Halls Locksmiths - Unlocking the Past

Halls Locksmiths and Security in Nottingham is the East Midlands premier locksmiths and security specialist company. The firm has been in business since the 1880s.

Today, from its showrooms at 88-92 Alfreton Road, Nottingham, the company offers all locksmith services, including coded key cutting, rim locks, mortise locks for wooden doors, UPVC door locks, aluminium door locks and all types of cabinet locks. All the major brands are stocked - Yale, Chubb, Assa, Abloy, Union, Era, and Kaba.

Key cutting from the largest range of key blanks in Nottingham, and indeed the East Midlands, is carried out by fully trained key locksmiths with 16 key machines kept busy cutting keys for all the major institutions in the area. Keys are also cut by automatic computerised machines whilst car keys are cut and coded while clients wait.

Security workshop work, including master key lock building, is carried out in-house by bench locksmiths; the work also includes lock repairs, lock manufacture, making keys to locks, making groups of locks fit the same key and many other tasks.

Halls is not however, just a locksmiths, the firm prides itself on being able to solve every kind of security problem from replacing locks due to a break in or lost keys, fitting or opening locks and safes to car key cutting and programming on site. Halls provides 24 hour locksmith services from a fleet of fully stocked vans. It offers free surveys for safes, access control, window grills, home security, and business security.

The firm was founded in 1885 by Clay Hall who opened the firm's first shop in Derby Road. Since that time the firm has expanded down the generations, providing its customers with all the latest gadgets for the home from gas fittings and iron stoves in the 1880s, to new lawn mowers in the 1910s to wireless in the 1920s and on to the modern security systems of the present day.

Though trained as a wheelwright, Clay Hall had a varied career, not least as a ship's carpenter. In 1866 he left the sea and became a publican as landlord of the Running Horse in Alfreton Road, later the Fox Hound Inn in Union Road, and subsequently the Bay Horse on Alfred Street.

Top left: Founder, Clay Hall. **Above:** *93 Derby Road pictured in 1890.* **Left:** *C. Hall & Sons Expanded after acquiring 95 Derby Road in 1900.*

In 1885 Clay Hall bought a small lock-up shop at 63A Derby Road. There Clay sold Sheffield cutlery, Japanese curios, plated cruets and teapots, and a little ironmongery.

The business had cost £40 to buy. The first week's takings were £2. Clay Hall's son Arthur was assistant and errand boy. Two years later the business moved to new and larger premises at 93 Derby Road where the family lived over the shop. Arthur's younger brother Albert now left school and join the growing family business.

The first shop had simply 'Clay Hall' above the window, now it was C.Hall & Sons. Before long the next door premises, number 95, were acquired for expansion, and with it came an increasing range of goods: air pistols, rifles, saucepans, kettles, motor cycle parts and locks. Surprisingly in today's regulated world the shop even stocked gunpowder. One use for gunpowder was the dangerous practice of clearing soot from blocked flues by dropping a screw of paper filled with the explosive into the shop stove and standing well back!

Clay Hall died in 1909 leaving his sons Arthur and Albert to run the business including a new branch in Beeston. Four years later however, Albert left to take up a partnership with an engineering firm in Derby leaving Arthur in sole ownership.

Just prior to the outbreak of the First World War there was a 'bicycle boom'. The shop window was now filled with cycle accessories; over 30 varieties of cycle lamps alone were stocked. Arthur was out to corner this new market. He was also a cycling enthusiast himself who thought nothing of touring Devon and Cornwall with his wife May for their two weeks annual holiday.

Arthur's son Lewis Hall eventually joined the firm as part-time delivery boy after school from 4.30 until 8pm. He was also expected to work all day Saturday from 8am until 10pm. One of his Saturday jobs was to deliver tins of petrol and paraffin in a handcart – his reward was sixpence, just two and a half pence in modern decimal currency.

In 1918 at the age of seventeen Lewis became manager of a new branch in Netherfield, whilst his elder brother Captain Cyril Hall, newly released from the Army, helped run the business from the main premises.

Wireless crystal sets made their appearance in the 1920s. Lewis opened a department covering this latest novelty. Two and then three valve radio receivers soon came along. Lewis built many radio sets from kits both at home and at work between serving customers - and actually sold them at the kit price. 'Wireless' was rather a misnomer however, given that many yards of wire were needed to make each radio receiver set.

Top left and left: Mr Clay Hall and his daughter take tea with son and daughter-in-law Mr and Mrs Albert Hall. Left: Arthur and wife May with their son Lewis. Above right: Capt. Cyril Hall, son of Arthur Hall. Below: Lewis Hall pictured at their Bulwell shop in 1925.

Having a wireless was not always helpful however. During the General Strike in 1926 the BBC News announcer reported that the strike would end that night. Lewis promptly chalked up the information outside the shop. Within minutes the notice had attracted a crowd of angry miners who tore the notice down and ripped it to shreds. Happily the miners were more considerate to Lewis.

During the Second World War Lewis' son Peter helped out as an errand boy and began to learn about locks from Arthur Hall who was recalled from semi-retirement as younger family members went off to 'do their bit' in the forces.

Arthur Hall died in 1946 and Cyril took over the Nottingham shop. In the following years the business would expand

its range of DIY goods and wood supplies. Opening locks and safes was also of increasing importance.

In 1962 the Beeston premises were sold and Cyril and Lewis Hall retired leaving Peter Hall as Managing Director. The firm now moved to new premises at 126-128 Derby Road. A decade later the firm moved again to even larger premises at 96 Derby Road.

During the 1970s locksmithing services grew in demand to such an extent that a separate locksmith company was formed with Peter's son Martin Clay appointed as director.

In 1983 such was the demand for locksmith work that the DIY section of Halls was phased out. Burglar alarms, CCTV and electric entry systems now became the order of the day. A much larger display of safes and locks, together with the expert advice of a trained team of locksmiths, was always available.

The team of locksmiths was led by Martin Clay Hall. Martin was a Fellow member of the Master Locksmiths' Association. Peter Hall became a Council Member of the Master Locksmiths' Association, a member of the Nottingham Crime Prevention Panel and a representative on the British Standards committee formulating British Standard BS 3621/1980 on security locks.

*Top left: 99 Derby Road in the 1950s. **Top right:** 126-128 Derby Road, 1962. **Left, both pictures:** C Hall & Sons' High Road (left), Beeston, shop in 1958 and Wollaton Road, Beeston, shop in 1960 (inset). **Above:** Lewis Hall cutting keys in the 1960s.*

progress which has been made as the company looks forward to another century of service.

Meanwhile, with a fine staff team including three retail operators, four service locksmiths and five office staff, Hall's is well placed to face the challenges of the future providing the people of Nottingham with the highest level of service, expertise and, above all, security.

In 1990 Peter Hall decided to retire and entrepreneur Harry Everington joined the company in partnership with Martin as joint shareholders. Harry's financial and business expertise helped steer the company forward opening a new shop in Derby in 1991. Unfortunately, the shop was closed following pedestrianisation of the area in 1993. The team of Martin as Managing Director, Paul Goulding as Contracts Director and Harry Everington then steadily increased the business through the millennium and into the 21st century, all the time adapting

Top left: *The team at Halls in the mid-1980s, Peter Hall is seated front right alongside his son Martin.* **Left:** *Hall's Locksmiths Safe and Security Centre in the 1980s.* **Above:** *Three generations of the Hall family pictured in 2009, from left to right: Peter Hall, Kathryn Hall, Joseph Hall and Martin Hall.* **Below:** *Halls Security Centre, 88-92 Alfreton Road, Nottingham, 2009.*

to the changing market, adding more CCTV and electronic security to the armoury of security devices. In 2005 Harry Everington resigned from the board leaving Martin in full control of the business.

Martin's daughter Kathryn joined the firm in 2005 as Company Secretary. In 2006 she decided to leave and study at university.

Joseph Hall joined the business in 2008 taking over from Kathryn as Contracts Co-ordinator, making him and his sister, the sixth generation of the Hall family working in the business.

After 125 years the Hall family is proud to continue what Clay Hall started back in 1885. He would surely be delighted by the

Willbond - Where Else?

For over a century, the firm of G B Willbond Ltd has been exceeding the expectations of loyal customers in the East Midlands. Today, proud to be independent – and not part of a faceless group – Willbond understands exactly what customers are looking for in plumbing supplies and bathrooms.

Willbond knows that its customers want and expect the highest quality, the widest selection and the best possible value. More than that, they want helpful and friendly advice. Since the firm first opened its doors over a hundred years ago this has been the key to its continued success.

Professional. Approachable. Knowledgeable. Friendly: that's what sets Willbond apart and makes all the difference to its customers.

Probably no one will ever know all of the various kinds of employment that George Baines Willbond undertook, but the local directories record at least three. In 1894 he was described as a 'canal boat and nuisance inspector', while the 1902 directory gave his profession as 'sanitary engineer'.

Some four years later he was similarly described, but by 1908 he had changed again and was now in business as a builders' merchant operating from the Midland Station yard, off Wollaton Road in Old Radford. The business evidently thrived. George B Willbond died in 1932 and left almost £10,000. His son, Harold Walter Willbond, then took over the business.

However, running a builder's merchants wasn't really Harold Willbond's cup of tea, and in 1941 he decided to put it up for sale. Frank Burrows, a director of Nottingham Mills Company, a firm of timber merchants, was advised by Lenton builder Harold Butler who was well placed to judge that G B Willbond was a good investment. Accordingly, even though it

was not quite their line of business Mr Burrows and his fellow directors E F Winser and W O Woodward decided to purchase the company for £900. Its location by the sidings at Radford station was extremely convenient, given that much of G B Willbond's building materials arrived by rail. With the gradual expansion of the business, additional storage was sought and a site was acquired in nearby St Peter's Street in 1947. This consisted of a yard and an old stable block. However, the purchase hit a snag. The stables already had a tenant. They could ask the occupant to leave but they were not entitled to evict his horse! A solicitor was consulted who only confirmed that the horse really was protected by the law and so G B Willbond's new owners, had to find the horse alternative stabling before they could move in.

A decision was taken to make G B Willbond a limited company in 1949. By 1953 a range of plumbing materials was added to the stocks. In the late 1950s the company had to start looking for a replacement for its St Peter's Street outlet when the City Council declared that part of Radford a redevelopment area. A site on Faraday Road was bought from the Gas Board and offices and warehousing built.

*Top: Where it all began as a builders merchant in Radford by George Baines Willbond - a Canal Boat and Nuisance Inspector. **Left:** Willbond becomes a limited company. **Below:** Willbond diversifies into plumbing supplies.*

storey office block – all in all an ideal HQ for a fast-growing business, where there was room for the expansion Tony Hogg planned. The year 1996 was the Willbond centenary and the company marked the occasion with a huge celebration for customers, suppliers and staff at the East Midlands Conference Centre. In the same year the Ilkeston Road premises were renovated, the design winning a Civic Trust Award. A new point of sale computer system was installed and a new Training Centre set up.

By now the company operated in three divisions, plumbing, heating and drainage equipment supplies to trade and retail, a

In 1961 the company opened for business in Faraday Road and the St Peter's Street outlet was sold to the Council. Plumbing supplies had gradually grown in importance and these were all kept at Faraday Road with the building materials still based in the station yard. Then, in the mid-seventies it was decided to stop trading in building materials and to close down the station yard. All efforts were concentrated on plumbing supplies at Faraday Road where additional land and properties had been gradually acquired. The operation there was expanded and, in 1978, a row of shops on Ilkeston Road was purchased and converted into bathroom and fitted kitchen showrooms.

When Managing Director Tony Hogg bought Willbond in 1987 he was determined to build on the company's impressive history and to grow the business across the East Midlands. He was also

determined to make it a 'young company' again and new directors were admitted to the board.

The Board was strengthened by the appointment in 1990 of Simon Chambers as Purchasing Director. He joined the very experienced Geoffrey Chibbett who was brought in to provide non-executive advice to the young management team.

Top: The specialist plumbers merchants branch opened in Faraday Road, Lenton, Nottingham by Willbond in 1961.
***Above:** The first Willbond specialist Kitchen & Bathroom Centre opens in Ilkeston Road, Nottingham in 1976.* ***Left:** Tony Hogg, Managing Director purchased the company in a management buy-out in 1987.* ***Below:** 1995 saw the company's plumbing supplies operation relocated to Deakins Place, Radford, Nottingham.*

An external sales team had also been recruited, and by the mid-1990s the company had outgrown its Faraday Road site.

Fortunately a very convenient relocation became available just around the corner in the shape of the former AS Toone premises on Deakins Place, St Peter's Street in Radford. Here the company acquired a two acre site, 40,000 square feet of storage and a two

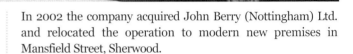

contracts division for larger jobs and the Kitchen and Bathroom Centre on Ilkeston Road.

In 2000 Tony Hogg managed to buy out his venture capital backers, 3i plc, and the company was once again a pure family-owned business.

By then however, road congestion was a fact of life in Nottingham and the East Midlands in general and it had become more difficult for customers to get through the traffic to the Willbond branches in Radford.

This called for a change in strategy and the Management Team determined that if the customers could not get to Willbond then Willbond must go to them via a local branch network.

Ray Wheatley was recruited as the new Branch Director and a hectic period of new branch openings ensued.

In 2002 the company acquired John Berry (Nottingham) Ltd. and relocated the operation to modern new premises in Mansfield Street, Sherwood.

The following year a new branch was established south of the River Trent off Melton Road West Bridgford to complete the Nottingham branch network.

By 2004 it was time to expand into Derbyshire and after many months searching for a new site the Company decided to buy a brown field site and build a superb new branch and showroom in a high profile location on London Road, Derby.

To coincide with the expansion into Derbyshire the company decided to close its Kitchens department and to focus its operations into two divisions, Willbond Plumbing Centres and Willbond Bathroom Centres each with its own distinctive livery and dedicated staffing.

During 2005 the company caught its breath and consolidated its position, with Geoffrey Chibbett retiring from the Board and Malcolm Evans taking his place as a Non-Executive Director.

Top left: In 1996 Willbond celebrated its centenary year and won a Civic Award for the refurbishment of its Kitchen & Bathroom Centre. Above: Willbond's Sherwood branch opened on Mansfield Street in 2002 the same year the company acquired Plumbers' Merchants John Berry (Nottm). Left: The company's West Bridgford branch which opened in Ludlow Hill Road in 2003.

four Bathroom Centres in eight separate locations across the East Midlands. A staff of over 80 people, each bursting with friendly professionalism, make conducting business with Willbond an easy and enjoyable experience for customers both old and new.

The main bulk of Willbond's business is with the trade but the company enjoys strong retail support at both its Plumbing Centres and its Bathroom Centres from customers that are delighted by its comprehensive stocks and competitive prices.

Today, 114 years after the business was founded, Tony Hogg and his team are still working hard to ensure that Willbond remains the supplier of choice for both trade and retail customers across the East Midlands.

By 2006 however, the company was back on the expansion trail with new Plumbing Centre openings in Ilkeston and Chesterfield.

The first branch opening in Lincolnshire came in 2007 with a combined Plumbing and Bathroom Centre established on the site of a former Peugeot dealership on London Road in Grantham. Now with three dedicated Bathroom Centres it was time to bolster the Board again: long-serving manager Lisa Jepson was deservedly promoted to Director in charge of the retail operations.

In 2008, two years after opening its Plumbing Centre in the town, the company acquired the assets of the Spital Tile Centre in Chesterfield and created another combined Plumbing and Bathroom Centre on the Spital Lane site. Today the company boasts seven Plumbing Centres and

Top left: Willbond's Derby branch and showroom on London Road. *Left:* The Ilkeston Plumbing Centre, opened in 2006. *Above:* Willbond's Grantham Plumbing and Bathroom Centre. *Below:* Spital Tiles acquired by Willbond in 2008.

Spring Lane Farm Shop
Real Food, Real People

With its fine selection of fresh local veg, fruit and meats, all from the Spencer family farm, the award-winning Spring Lane Farm Shop at Mapperley Plains enjoys a reputation second to none.

The family run retail business with its fine, friendly staff stocks home-produced and locally-produced goods ranging from fruit and vegetables, meat butchered on the premises to bread, eggs, cheeses and many delicious luxury goods.

Home-produced beef, local lamb and local pork are available alongside a wide range of homemade sausages to choose from: plain pork, pork & mustard, pork & black pudding, not forgetting sweet chilli and hickory smoked sausages. The family firm makes all of its own beef burgers, pork & apple burgers and lamb burgers and specialises in barbecue meats for the summer months.

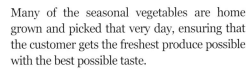

The Butchery team will always try their very best to cater for every customer's needs.

The shelves are always stocked with a wide range of locally-produced seasonal vegetables. A wide choice of jams and preserves, as well as local honey is also available.

Many of the seasonal vegetables are home grown and picked that very day, ensuring that the customer gets the freshest produce possible with the best possible taste.

Cauliflowers, broccoli and brussel sprouts are cut on the morning of sale. Carrots, leeks, cabbage and parsnips are grown on one of the neighbouring farms.

All the potatoes in the shop are grown and produced by Spring Lane Farm itself. The very best varieties are carefully selected to give customers a potato with a great taste, high quality and at the right price.

A flock of free range hens produces eggs for the shop, and are often sold the same day that they are laid.

Above: Views of Herbert Spencer on the farm in the 1940s.
Below left: A letter of appreciation to Spring Lane Farm from Nottinghamshire Agricultural Executive in the cause for food production in the post war years. Below: Herbert and Cyril (on the tractor) with Albert Holmes in the 1940s.

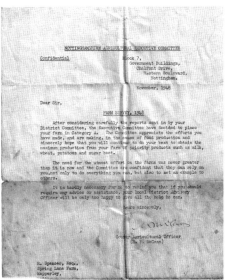

Elsewhere in the shop a large range of English cheeses is available including the three main Blue Stiltons from Cropwell Bishop, Colston Basset and Long Clawson. Also stocked are a few continental varieties including Old Amsterdam, Dolcelatte and Jarlsberg.

Meanwhile the cooked meat counter boasts many fine meats, most of them cooked on the premises. These include roast beef and roast pork as well as ox tongue and pickled brisket, not to mention the Spring Lane Farm's prize-winning ham, twice given a Gold Star rating by the Guild of Fine Food.

More recently a bakery has been added where fresh bread and cakes are made. Using the best Rank Hovis flour, the bakery makes all varieties including white, wholemeal, granary and Hovis bread, not to mention Spring Lane's very own meat pies, sausage rolls and pasties.

But how did all this gastronomic glory come about? The story goes back many years indeed. Spring Lane Farm, and more recently its famed farm shop, have been run by three generations of the Spencer family, spanning a period of over 70 years.

Herbert Spencer was born on 26 September, 1916 and died on 5 May, 1993. He was born in Hayfield, Derbyshire.

Moving to Cripwell Farm in Wymeswold, Leicestershire, just after World War One Herbert was the eldest son in his family and was educated at the village school in Wymeswold. He took what was then the equivalent of his 'eleven plus' along with two other boys in his class, and went on to Loughborough Grammar School. On his way to school each day, one of his first jobs was to take the mare and the milk float half a mile down the road to put the churns on the milk stand, and then unhitch the mare and put her out to graze.

Herbert subsequently passed the entrance exams to go on to Oxford University, but could not go because of lack of money during the Depression of the late 1920s. No matter - all Herbert really wanted to do was to farm, but his father could not afford to keep him at home, so instead Herbert took up painting and decorating with an uncle.

*Top: An early view of Spring Lane Farm Shop. **Above:** Cyril and Herbert on Spring Lane Farm in 1964, preparing for hay making.*

Over the following years Herbert saved as much money as possible for when the opportunity came to acquire a farm of his own. There were two farms available in Wymeswold on a tenancy basis, but then Herbert heard about Spring Lane Farm in Nottinghamshire, about to become available to buy. The land however, was classified only as 'Grade C' which Herbert knew that would be hard work to bring it back up to Grade A status.

In 1939 on the eve of war, and despite worries about the land which might take years of labour to bring up to a high standard, Herbert decided to take on the challenge and move to Spring Lane Farm. That same year he met a lovely young girl called Edna May Holmes.

On 8 September, 1939, Herbert acquired the tenancy at Spring Lane Farm. With it came six cows and a horse called Blossom. After the purchase he had just £10 left to his name!

In those early days, Herbert did all the milking by hand and transported it to Woods Dairy (on Ranson Road) using an old converted motorbike and side-car; the original side-car had been replaced with a platform to stand the milk churns on.

After 1947 the Milk Marketing Board was in operation, and thereafter the milk would be collected from the farm, making life a little easier.

In the meantime however, Herbert had married Edna May Holmes in 1940. Four years later they welcomed their son Cyril into the world - whom they hoped would one day become the second generation to run the farm.

Horse power not horses was the face of the future. Mechanisation was the way forward, and in 1947 Herbert invested £225 in his first tractor, a Fordson with registration FNN517; this cost the princely sum of £1 per year to insure.

Above: Cyril seeing to the cows in his early years. Below: Cyril and the family dog on the farm in the 1990s.

The business began to grow. By 1953 Spring Lane Farm was milking 25 cows by: machine, producing three acres of potatoes, and had 50 laying hens - all with one workman. The future looked bright.

When young Cyril Spencer left Robert Mellors School in Arnold, he returned to work on the family farm. In 1968 he married Dorothy Horspool and went into partnership with his father by investing £500 in the business.

The dairy herd now increased from 34 cows to 60 and a new yard and milking parlour were built.

Towards the end of the 1970s Dorothy Spencer started selling the home-grown potatoes and freshly laid eggs from the farmhouse doorstep... her entrepreneurship was to be the origin of Spring Lane Farm Shop.

The next generation of the farming family - Mark Steven Spencer - was born in 1970, and after attending Col. Frank Seeley School in Calverton and Shuttleworth Agricultural College, he too returned home to work at Spring Lane Farm.

During the 1990s Spring Lane Farm increased its size to over 200 acres. A new Farm Shop was built in November, 1992, selling vegetables, potatoes, eggs and other local produce. Mark Spencer was involved in increasing the dairy herd to its maximum size and soon a brand new milking parlour was installed to cope with this expansion. The Spring Lane herd soon acquired pedigree status, producing many cow families from home breeding.

Mark went into partnership with his father Cyril in 1995, forming C H Spencer & Son. The following year Mark met and married Claire Hickling: their daughter Jessica was born in 1997 the fourth generation of the family at the farm. Meanwhile Claire would help out with the Farm Shop and with the bookwork.

In November 2000 came a son, Charles (Charlie) Henry Spencer. By the age of five years old Charlie had already decided that he wanted to be a farmer when grown up.

By the early 2000s however, the dairy industry had hit an all time low, and a decision was made to cease milk production at the farm, and expand the shop.

In November 2003 the current incarnation of the Spring Lane Farm Shop, now incorporating a Butchery and Cheese Counter, opened its doors for the first time. Thanks to the 26 dedicated

and hardworking staff that help the shop to run as smoothly as possible, and to the many regular customers whose word-of-mouth has spread the shop's reputation far and wide, the business is thriving.

But if anyone thinks it could be even better the Spencer family is always happy to hear customers' ideas and suggestions; so please don't hesitate to speak to any member of the friendly family team!

Top: Mark Spencer checking the cabbages. Centre: Baker, Paul (left), with the farm's delicious pork pies and Head Butcher, Brian (right), at work behind the meat counter. Below left: Young Charlie tending to the brussell sprouts. Below: Three generations of the Spencer family, Cyril (right), Mark (left) and Charlie.

A.W. Lymn - The Family Funeral Service

As the Romans had it 'Tempus fugit' - time flies. Time speeds by for all of us, and sooner or later we will all need the help of a funeral director. Although there may be new businesses which can provide such services, somehow it never seems quite right, even disrespectful, to make use of a firm which has not acquired the patina of age, that indefinable degree of dignity which can only be gained through having been around for a long time.

In Nottingham A.W. Lymn The Family Furneral Service, the well known firm of funeral directors, has long been associated with the city. The company's head office is still located in Sneinton just a few hundred yards from Goosegate, where its founders, Arthur William Lymn and his son Harold, once traded as furniture makers and dealers. In 1907 father and son decided to specialise in the manufacture and supply of coffins and the provision of a full funeral service, hence their entry into the 'undertaking' profession as it was most commonly known in

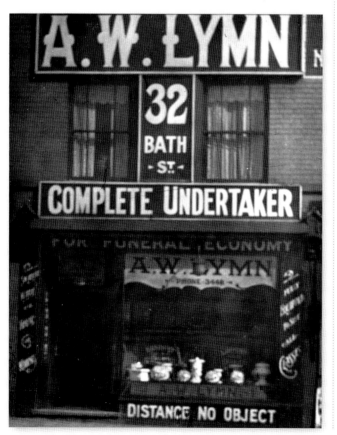

those days. Before long the new business was soon so successful that it had to move to larger premises. In 1915 the office was moved to Bath Street, opposite Sneinton Market. The firm's horses were stabled in Robin Hood Street and coffins manufactured in Handel Street. The stables were eventually replaced with garaging for motor vehicles; the same site which now houses an impressive array of

silver-grey Rolls-Royce hearses and limousines, reputed to be the largest fleet of such vehicles in the world. When Arthur Lymn himself died in 1929 control of the business passed to his widow Louisa and his son Harold. In 1939, close to the outbreak of the second world war, Louisa died and Harold took sole charge. The business continued to grow despite the outbreak of war- even though during the war years horses had to be reintroduced as a consequence of petrol rationing. Harold himself was involved in the war effort serving as a volunteer at the Civil Defence mortuary.

Top left: Arthur William Lymn. *Left:* 32 Bath Street, where the office moved to in 1915. *Above:* Two early views of A.W. Lymn's Robin Hood Street premises. *Below:* A 1930s Rolls-Royce hearse.

In subsequent years Harold's son Douglas (now deceased) and son-in-law George Rose continued to develop the business which became a limited company in 1958. Douglas and George became Members of the British Institute of Embalmers and were involved in the first repatriation of human remains from England to Pakistan at about this time.

In 1977 the company moved its headquarters to Robin Hood House in Robin Hood Street where the main hub of the firm is still to be found.

George Rose and his wife Sheila (Harold's daughter) are now retired but still take an active interest in the business. Their son Nigel Lymn Rose and daughter Jackie Lymn Rose now manage the business on a daily basis assisted by their grandchildren Chloe and Matthew Lymn Rose. Ernest Smith's, the company's monumental masonry division, which was founded by Harold Lymn is now run by George and Sheila's daughter-in-law Penny Lymn Rose and grandson Ben Percival.

By 2004 there would be no fewer than 22 funeral homes serving the whole of Nottinghamshire and southern Derbyshire, as well as an in-house floristry division City Flowers and the memorial masons Ernest Smith. The company is a Member of the National Association of Funeral Directors and boasts more holders of the Diploma in Funeral Directing awarded by the Association than any other family owned funeral business in the country. The company is also a member, by invitation, of the prestigious American Organisation of Selected Independent Funeral Homes. All the multi-cultural and multi-faith requirements of its citizens are addressed by A.W. Lymn The Family Furneral Service. All budgets are catered for, regardless of the means of the individuals concerned and every funeral that is carried out is conducted in the most dignified, professional and respectful manner possible.

In 2007 the firm celebrated its centenary. To mark this occasion the A.W. Lymn Centenary Foundation was established, a charitable trust continually financed by the firm with the objective of helping those in the community whose special needs cannot be funded from elsewhere. And whilst time still flies A.W. Lymn maintains the tradition of a horse drawn hearse and mourners coaches as an alternative to modern motor vehicles.

Above, left and right: Early funerals conducted by the company. ***Below left:*** *The impressive A.W. Lymn fleet of Rolls-Royce's.* ***Below:*** *The Lymn family outside Robin Hood House on Sunday 19th August 2007 when they held an open day to the general public to celebrate their centenary.*

Myford Ltd - Engineering Excellence

Myford Engineering (now Myford Limited) was founded in September 1934, by the late Cecil Moore. Still based at its original site in Wilmot Lane, Beeston, the company is now led by the founder's grandson Christopher Moore.

Cecil had originally worked in the lace trade as a twist hand. After the 1914-18 war, when Cecil was settled down to married life, he had a well equipped workshop at home featuring a treadle-powered Drummond lathe, a hand shaping machine, and a small hand operated drilling machine. Here he used to manufacture spare parts for motorcycles and cars. When time permitted, he would also build the odd Stuart Turner model stationary engine.

Around 1930, Cecil Moore went into partnership with a local man named Winfield to build a small lathe. Cecil did all the design work, and made the foundry patterns in his workshop. The pair set up business in Beeston, renting a room on the top floor of Neville's factory. In 1934, Cecil struck out on his own, renting another room in Neville's factory, and began trading as Myford, which was Cecil's paternal grandmother's maiden name.

The firm made small metal working lathes, the ML1, ML2, ML3 and ML4. An ML4, the deluxe model, would have sold for £7.00. Myford also made lathes for other people, notably Gamages, their lathe sold for £3. 10s and the Zyto for S. Tysack and Sons.

On the outbreak of the second world war Myford was manufacturing the ML4. The Ministry of Supply wanted the Drummond 'M' Type and Myford was instructed to purchase the 'M' Type business from Drummond Bros. The company was also commissioned to make small capstan lathes, and valve re-facing machines for Churchill and Black & Decker.

Myford launched a brand new lathe in 1946, the ML7. The ML7 incorporated the latest thinking and technology, and was unique in that, all pulleys and gears

Top left: *Cecil Moore, co-founder of Myford.* **Left:** *Once a local landmark, Neville's Lace Mill where Cecil Moore originally started his business in 1934.* **Above:** *A late version of the ML7 lathe, produced from 1946 to 1977.*

Parallel to this the company also manufactures the MG12 range of high precision, cylindrical grinding machines. The five model range runs from a manual model through to a hydraulic plunge feed machine with automatic cycles, all of which enjoy a much-coveted reputation for quality and longevity.

Cecil Moore's grandson Christopher Moore joined the company in 1971 and is now Managing Director and Chairman. The company is still very much a family business and Christopher is very appreciative of the family's support. Adhering to long held policies of continuous development and improvement in both quality of product and management, the firm remains strong and competitive.

Today Myford sells machines across the globe, with up to 45% of output going to export. Adhering to a strict policy of producing accurate and well finished machines, Myford's is able to compete with the best products in the world, despite stiff new competition from the Far East.

Myford Ltd is proud, that world over, the company name is held up as a symbol of precision and performance.

were guarded. The ML7 was launched at £34.00 when the Myford Drummond 'M' Type sold for £42.00. The ML7 became a world beating lathe, with 500 a month being produced in the early days. Production finally ended in 1977. The ML7 was followed in 1947 by the MG9, a small cylindrical grinding machine. A year later came the ML8 a multi purpose woodworking lathe produced until 1989. In 1953 the Super 7 lathe arrived, still in production today, and in 1956 the first MG12 cylindrical grinding machine.

Top left: Mr John Moore pictured alongside a Myford Super 7 Conoisseur. **Left:** *Myford products, a lathe (left), grinder (centre) and milling machine.* **Below:** *A Myford 10/258 Super 7 Connoisseur lathe, mounted on an industrial stand, with optional rear splash guard and safe work light.*

Cecil's son, John Moore, had joined the company in 1947, having spent the war years working on the design side at Rolls Royce, and ending up working on the early Gas Turbine Engines at the Barnoldswick Factory. John followed his father, becoming Managing Director and then Chairman before retiring in 1987. Despite his so-called retirement however, John continued to take a keen interest in the company, managing numerous design projects right up until his 85th year. In 1999 John headed a design team with the brief to improve the spindle capacity of the ever-popular Super 7 range of lathes: 2001 saw the launch of the much improved Super 7 Plus range. Produced by a loyal and conscientious workforce the range-topping Super 7B Connoisseur continues to be the firm's best selling product.

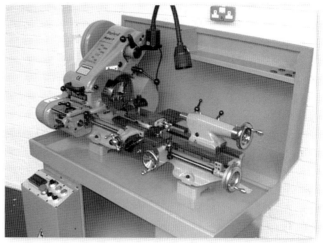

Hawthornes Printers - A Century of Integrity

The grandfather of the founder of Hawthornes of Nottingham Ltd, Reverend Charles Oliver Hawthorne, was a Wesleyan Minister. A tradition of integrity has been passed down through the Hawthorne family.

John Ranshall Hawthorne established a stationery and printing business in Goldsmith Street, Nottingham in 1895. Ten years later he moved to Clumber Street, where J.R. Hawthorne's son, Ranshall Thomas Oliver joined him in 1911. When JR died in 1927, RTO agreed with the rest of the family to buy the business for £2,300.

A separate printing works opened in Goose Gate, Hockley in 1933-4. An additional shop was opened in Radford Road in 1937, followed by yet another, in Mansfield Road four years later. By then the Printing Works had moved to Maypole Yard (off Clumber Street).

Richard Hawthorne joined the firm in 1947 and the next year saw the opening of another shop in Bath Street, Ilkeston.

Throughout the late 1940s and early 1950s RTO displayed a flair for publicity, particularly in ways of displaying greeting cards. Mainly in the hands of Richard Hawthorne and David Hind, the business was consolidated under one roof by a move to Palm Street, New Basford, Nottingham in 1961. Now instead of being a stationery retailer with its own printing facility, the company became a printer which also sold commercial stationery, office furniture and safes.

Chris Hawthorne rejoined the company in 1966 after two and a half years experience in printing in Canada and became Managing Director in 1973.

The first full colour printing press was installed in 1975 beginning the move for the company to become 100% printing. The 1970s and 1980s also saw the acquisition of Fyson Brothers (Bulwell) Ltd in Nottingham and John S Speight Ltd in Guiseley, Yorkshire. Extra premises were bought in Palm Street to accommodate a progressive installation of multi-colour printing presses. In 1993 the first press costing over one million pound was bought.

Hawthornes still operates at the site in New Basford and is now one of the leading sheet fed printers in the UK with 24 hour production, specialising in high quality printing, working in colour-critical markets. The current Directors, Paul Hackett (Managing), Steve Broxham (Finance) and Chris Hawthorne (Chairman) are committed to growth through adding multi-media and other services to Hawthornes' printing facilities.

Top: The founder John Ranshall Hawthorne. **Left:** *A picture of the Clumber Street premises shortly after it had opened.* **Above:** *Hawthornes' Palm Street premises.*

Picture The Past

In the past, anyone wanting to view the collections of hundreds of thousands of old images in the libraries and museums of Nottinghamshire or Derbyshire would have had to travel many miles to try and track down the ones they were interested in. This proved to be frustrating and time consuming for researchers, a barrier to anyone from further a field as well as damaging to the more fragile images from all the handling. The collections include photographs, slides, negatives, glass plates, postcards and engravings recalling the history of our local communities for a hundred years and more.

Thankfully senior staff in four local authorities got their heads together to solve the problem and the idea of conserving the images using digitisation whilst at the same time giving people all over the world access to the digitised versions was conceived. Funding was obtained from the Heritage Lottery Fund at the beginning of 2002 together with additional cash from the four partner authorities, Nottinghamshire and Derbyshire County Councils and the City Councils of Nottingham and Derby. Local studies staff in the libraries and museums started collating images and information ready for inclusion in the project and sent out thousands of letters requesting copyright clearance from the original photographers or their relatives. Nick Tomlinson was appointed as project manager to lead a team of experienced professionals inputting the information into a custom-built database and carefully digitising the images.

The Picture the Past website (www.picturethepast.org.uk) was launched in June 2003 and currently holds in excess of 76,000 pictures. It now attracts well over 10,000 visitors every month from all over the world viewing thousands of pages of images. The site is updated on a regular basis and actually gives the user the ability to 'correct' existing information or add more information to those pictures with scant details.

The website is designed to be as 'easy to use' as possible and includes a simple keyword search facility as well as more comprehensive search mechanisms for users looking for images with a particular theme or by a specific photographer. Visitors can print out low resolution copies for their own personal use or study purposes but for those users wanting to own a top quality glossy photographic copy the website includes an on-line ordering service. Thanks to the involvement of Derby Evening Telegraph this enables users to browse the collection and order and pay for their selections securely on-line. The prints are produced on state-of-the-art equipment and, as a non-profit making project, all the income raised from this service goes back into the conservation and preservation of more original pictures. This book gives you the chance to sample just a handful of the images contained in the website and it is very much hoped that you will go on to enjoy the rest of the pictures on the website. For people who do not have access to the Internet at home, or who are not sure where to start, there are computers available for public use in all libraries and the local studies staff are more than willing to help you get started.

The website can be viewed at www.picturethepast.org.uk

Picture the Past makes historic images from the library & museum collections of Derby, Derbyshire, Nottingham & Nottinghamshire, freely available at the click of a mouse button.

ACKNOWLEDGMENTS

The publishers would like to sincerely thank a number of individuals and organisations for their help and contribution to this publication.

This book would have been almost impossible without the kind co-operation of the following:

www.picturethepast.org.uk

Nottingham Evening Post, Nottinghamshire County Council, Nottinghamshire Historical Film Unit,

Derbyshire Local Studies Libraries, The Cecil Brown Collection, L Cripwell, Nottingham City Council,

J Snowden, Edgar Lloyd, George L Roberts, G F Campion, H B Priestley, L Brownlow, Reg Baker,

Nottingham Girl Guides Association

Nottingham Evening Post

BYGONES, the Evening Post's monthly nostalgia magazine, which has been running since 1997, regularly features the sort of photographs you found in this book.

The magazine covers all sorts of subjects from Nottingham's past: royal visits, life in the inner city suburbs like The Meadows, Sneinton and St Ann's before redevelopment, old pubs, railways, trams and buses; Raleigh, Boots and Players.

Many of the photographs come from our archives, others from our friends at picturethepast.org.uk and many more, together with fascinating stories and memories, from our loyal readers.

Bygones is available, from local newsagents, priced 65p. Look out for our distinctive front cover.

To order a regular copy, call our Subscriptions Department on 0115 948 2000.

Press Association Images